THE REAL DEAL

THE REAL DEAL

A SPIRITUAL GUIDE
FOR BLACK TEEN GIRLS

BILLIE MONTGOMERY COOK

Judson Press
Valley Forge

THE REAL DEAL: A SPIRITUAL GUIDE FOR BLACK TEEN GIRLS

Judson Press has made every effort to trace the ownership of all quotes. In the event of a question arising from the use of a quote, we regret any error made and will be pleased to make the necessary correction in future printings and editions of this book.

Bible quotations in this volume are from the following versions of the Holy Bible:

New International Version, copyright © 1973, 1978, 1984. Used by permission of Zondervan Publishing House. (NIV)

The Living Bible, copyright © 1971. Used by permission of Tyndale House Publishers, Inc., Wheaton, IL 60189. All rights reserved. (TLB)

Contemporary English Version, copyright © 1991, 1992, 1995 by American Bible Society. Used by permission. (CEV)

New Revised Standard Version of the Bible, copyright © 1989 by the Division of Christian Education of the National Council of the Churches of Christ in the United States of America. Used by permission. All rights reserved. (NRSV)

The Holy Bible, King James Version (KJV)

ISBN-13: 978-0-7394-4358-3

Printed in the U.S.A.

To Jeanina
Always My "Boo"

"Be strong and courageous. Do not be terrified;
do not be discouraged, for the LORD your God will be
with you wherever you go...." (Joshua 1:9, NIV)

CONTENTS

PREFACE   ix
ACKNOWLEDGEMENTS   xiii
INTRODUCTION: What Is the Real Deal?   xvii

PART ONE: The Real Deal on Good Temple Design
  1. Self-esteem: Yes, You *Are* All of That!   3
  2. Truth: To Know That You Know That You Know   10
  3. Gratitude: Stop! Thank-you Time!   15
  4. Faith: Go, Darlin'! Go, Darlin'! Keep Your Head
     Up! Keep Your Head Up!   19
  5. Hope: Hold On—Tight!   25
  6. Love: Your Temple's Security and Alarm System   30

PART TWO: The Real Deal on Constructing Your Temple
  7. Friendship: One or Two Real Ones Will Do
     Just Fine   39
  8. Knowledge: Answers to the "Why" Questions
     of Life   43
  9. Spiritual Discipline: Buckle Up! Life's Roller
     Coaster Gets Bumpy Sometimes   50
 10. P.U.S.H.: Pray Until Something Happens   54
 11. Work: Bees Do It, Ants Do It...   59

PART THREE: The Real Deal on Challenges to Construction

12. Ingratitude: Don't Get Caught in This Trap!   67
13. Revenge: Don't Even Think about It!   73
14. Negativity: Pigeons Aren't the Only Ones
    That Will Drop Stuff on Your Temple!   79
15. Insecurity, Part I: "Too Blessed to Be Stressed"   84
16. Insecurity, Part II: Separating the "Paper Dolls"
    from the REAL WOMEN of God!   91
17. Sex and Sexuality: OK, Darlin', This Is the
    Real Deal!   96
18. Fear: Whom Are You Worshiping?   102
19. Suicide: Don't Believe the Hype!   107
20. Lack of Confidence in God: Let Dad
    Make It Better   113

LAST PART: The Real Deal on Finishing Touches for
Your Temple
Conclusion   121

PREFACE

My Dear One,

Welcome to the teenage years! What a mysterious and wondrous time for you, the teen—but such a scary and apprehensive time for parents. So many new and exciting things begin at this time. Your physical, social, psychological, and spiritual development will take on new meaning and leave you searching for answers to all kinds of questions. For some of the questions, parents have ready, predetermined, almost "stock" answers, because life, age, and experience have taught us well. For other questions, we fall silent, for we are just as stumped as you are.

Unlike our generation, you and your peers are bombarded daily with a relentless stream of media—television, radio, CDs, books, magazines, movies, music videos, the Internet, etc. All are selling something that does not exist through those mediums: the quickest, fastest way to happiness, thinness, sex appeal, beauty, longevity—and love.

How do God's great love and the lessons of Scripture get heard while the noise of the culture, of "the world," tries so hard to drown it out? How do we as parents, adults, and significant loved ones in your life make ourselves available to you when you need us—even as you attempt *not* to need us? How might we equip and arm you for independence while resisting the urge to bind your feet in umbilical cord and keep you out of harm's way? How can we shrink-wrap you in God's Word so that you will stand strong and firm when other forces surround you and try to test the strength of our teaching? Will you see your spiritual development as an awesome and important journey, or will you become impatient at its pace? Will you see it as something that applies to others but not to you? Will you speak as a fledgling young woman of God and then "walk the walk"? Or will you find it easier to just walk away?

These pages are given to you. They are the pearls from God's Word that are worth any price to possess—the things that as parents rest in our hearts that sometimes fail to come from our mouths. So many of the things about life—your body, love, dating, sexuality (got to talk about that!), relationships, friendships, hard times, harder times, your spiritual growth, and your sense of who you are…so many of the kinds of things that build a strong foundation for who you will become and what your spiritual temple will be—those things that must be said are collected here for you.

Sometimes these topics are mentioned and you don't want to hear them. Sometimes hurt and anger on both of our parts stand in the way of calm and clarity. Oftentimes it seems teens and adults share a common atmosphere but live on two very different planets.

But, from one planet to another, know that you are loved and prayed for every day—sometimes all day, without ceasing! Believe me: it can be done and it *is* done. Prayer is all that we as parents truly have to give to you. And, since prayer is God's power, it is all that is needed. We see so much intelligence, talent, creativity, energy, joy, and promise within you. Please give God the opportunity to show you what the Holy Spirit has shown to so many of us.

Take these words held here, be blessed, and know that they are of love and of God.

Always,
BMC

ACKNOWLEDGMENTS

Any and all acknowledgments of things accomplished within these pages must begin with praise and a grateful heart to God. It is God who chooses to rouse me early from great sleep and warm bed to walk and talk with him daily—friend to friend, boss to worker, father to daughter. There are no words for the glory, honor, and praise due him. Great has been the Lord's faithfulness to me.

Even at the launching of a first book, no words adequately convey—or even come close to conveying—all that I feel in my heart and spirit as I hold these pages in my hands. The simple words "Thank you" seem so meager, but they are spoken from my heart. And since this proverbial "15 minutes" may never come again, I shall use every second of it to give thanks and praise to God for the people he has so generously and lovingly placed in my life.

To my parents, "Bert and Bill," who have tried to live as examples before us, your children. Your prayers, patience, unconditional love, care, and giving make us who we are today. Yes, God is still working on us, but eternal thanks to you for introducing us to him—and for making that introduction an early one in our lives. Words fail but tears of gratitude make this paper soggy! Thank you.

To Nina, Dennis, Stanley, and the rest of the Mont-gomery/Cook/West "Crew" and "Posse." You know who you are and what you mean to me. Much love and God's richest blessings to one and all.

To Steph and Rae, who have been like "shade trees along the river bank." You have been there—always—to lift me when I weakened, to push me forward when I faltered, and to love me when it was hard for me to love myself. Thank you. (And yes, the paper gets soggier!)

To Jan, Katreena, Grace, John, and Dorothy; to Carolyn, GW, Syd, and Noe. All of you have faithfully cheered from the sidelines—even when the cheering was difficult to do. Thank you.

To Hattie, who pointed me in the direction of my spiritual gifts and who continues to grow toward her own. Thank you.

To Deni, who has taught me the truth about grace, courage, and empathy. Thank you for standing in the gap when others fail to see or get "it."

To Calvary, East Orange, New Jersery, for loving me and standing at the birthing table when creativity was born. To Mt. Pleasant, Norfolk, Virginia, for compelling me to grow in God's Word and teaching me to accept his will for our lives. It continues to be a joy and a wonder to see and watch the Lord work. Yes, thank you.

To Pastor Robert Culp, who demonstrated what it means to be a true shepherd when I was in need of one. Your words still hold true and have kept me, lo, these many years. Thank you—and God's continued blessings upon you and your fold.

To my pastor, Dr. Joe B. Fleming, for your faith in me and encouragement even when you didn't have a clue about what I wanted to do through my "projects." You've challenged us to give of ourselves and to trust God's reputation—no matter the circumstances. Thanks to you for being there for me and for my family—and love to your family.

To my Third Baptist Church family, who through your nurturing, support, and love have caused me to grow while learning to give God the praise for all things—on a daily basis. To Deacon Mary Hall and the Centennial Sunday School Class, who saw more in me than I ever saw within myself. You were there when times were hard but your strength and laughter kept me going. To members of the TBC Drama Ministry; your willingness to encourage me to try new things continues to inspire and challenge me. And to the faithful ones at Wednesday Night Prayer Meeting, who have allowed me to "bathe in and soak up" your testimonies and prayers—never erase me from the "list"! I thank God for all of you.

To Randy Frame, acquisitions editor at Judson Press, for not releasing his grip on a dream and for giving a new voice the opportunity to join the boisterous chorus of writers who have been singing for a while—my sincerest thanks. To Rebecca Irwin-Diehl, who has helped to get the "interior" design of this temple in great shape—thank you. And to the "worker bees" at Judson, thank you also.

Jeanina, read the first page. Joseph, continue to stay on the path. Let God show both of you how it pays to serve him. You will never regret it. Thank you for teaching me what it really means to be a mom. I love and pray for you daily.

And to Keith, my husband, head cheerleader, spiritual leader, confidante, and friend. Thank you for teaching me what 1 Corinthians 13 looks and feels like when a husband, man, and child of God lives it and doesn't just talk about it (especially the longsuffering part)! Yes, I got exactly what God planned for me. It is a joy and a blessing to have you and the children in my life.

Finally, to those who will pick this book up for any number of reasons (to browse, purchase, or critique), please know that God is real and that his plans for us defy our logic, reason, and understanding. How blessed we are to have a Father who loves us, just because...he's God.

Thank you all again. I love you, and God bless us, every one!

Billie

INTRODUCTION

WHAT IS THE REAL DEAL?

My Dear One,

What is *The Real Deal: A Spiritual Guide for Black Teen Girls*? It is the truth about who you are as a teen, a developing young black woman, a child of God, the daughter of our heavenly Father. It is a reality check against many of the questionable things that our culture tries to convince you to think, feel, and believe about yourself.

The Real Deal emphasizes the importance of building a relationship—your spiritual temple—with God, much like a contractor would build a physical structure. In each chapter, the process for building your temple is expressed through letters, prayers ("A Prayer for You"), and questions ("For Your Consideration"). There is also a place for your thoughts ("A Prayer from You").

A contractor prepares for building by gathering the right tools and the blueprints of the structure to be built. You must do the same. Keep your Bible handy—and don't tell me you don't have *that* critical tool and blueprint! The King James Version (KJV), New International Version (NIV), New Revised Standard Version (NRSV), The Living Bible (TLB), or Contemporary English Version (CEV) are good choices, and all are used throughout this text. (Note the initials at the end of the Scripture passages.)

The contractor would take special care to make sure the foundation for the building under construction was a strong, sturdy, and secure one. You must make sure the foundation of your temple has the same kind of strength, sturdiness, security, and durability (Part One: The Real Deal on Good Temple Design).

Just as the contractor's project progresses as the wiring, plumbing, roof, and walls go up, so should your temple progress as you grow in wisdom and maturity (Part Two: The Real Deal on Constructing Your Temple). From time to time, the contractor may experience problems and setbacks, unforeseen when the project was begun. You too will realize similar obstacles in your growth (Part Three: The Real Deal on Challenges to Construction).

But finally, the contractor rejoices in completion of the project by putting out the welcome mat and celebrating with a grand-opening, ribbon-cutting ceremony. You will experience the same as you grow to welcome into your temple the presence of God, his Son, Jesus Christ, and the Holy Spirit (Conclusion: The Real Deal on Finishing Touches for Your Temple).

As you turn these pages, keep that image in your head: one of working, building, learning, growing, and experiencing setbacks, but ultimately celebrating greater triumphs in the days ahead.

There is a great deal of work to do. Tools ready? Let us begin!

PART ONE

ON GOOD
TEMPLE DESIGN

1

SELF-ESTEEM

YES, YOU ARE ALL OF THAT!

Don't you know that you yourselves are God's temple and that God's spirit lives in you? If anyone destroys God's temple, God will destroy him; for God's temple is sacred, and you are that temple.... (1 Corinthians 3:16-17, NIV)

My Dear One,

We begin at the beginning, the basic design and foundation of the structure of your temple—the real deal about *who* you are and *whose* you are.

Understand that when you look at yourself in the mirror you are looking at a wonder. Take note of the young black face that you see reflected there. As you study the history of this country in school, read between the lines of the texts. African American history is not studied as much as it should be. (Remember: February is the shortest month of the year!) You must read and educate yourself about our people. You must be aware of the fact that one of the desired results of slavery was to have been the

3

complete elimination of black people from this country. We were supposed to die from being overworked. Just as animals die from exhaustion and exertion, such was to be our fate.

To see your reflection is to see that God had an entirely different game plan. Despite the best efforts of human beings through slavery, racism, oppression, segregation, and even death, we as a people, and you as an individual, are still here. Take a minute and think about that.

The current crop of women's magazines tell you that what you see in the mirror looking back at you is a mistake… a compilation of errors that must be corrected—to their specifications. They dictate that your lips are probably too large, nose too wide, hair too nappy, skin and hair too dark, hips too big, breasts not large enough, behind too broad. You are a young black woman. According to them, there's not too much beauty in being who you are.

What they don't tell you is that you are a child of God. You are "fearfully and wonderfully made" (Psalm 139:14, NIV). They also don't tell you that the body they dissect is greater than the sum of all of its parts. You are all that has been. Those lips are not just too big lips; those legs are not just too big legs; those hips are not just too big hips! Those lips, legs, and hips are your great-great-grand parents and great-aunts, -uncles, cousins, and other relatives…your ancestors of long ago! To deny the wonder of your body's features is to deny all that they were and all that you are!

The magazines and "fashion police" also don't tell you that those hips, legs, arms, and thighs house something still greater. They are the outer shell, the frame, the exterior that holds God's Spirit. Your body is the temple of God. It is where he lives. God does not pick just any old place in which to dwell. The Lord picks only the best of sites.

When a young woman accepts Christ as Lord and Savior of her life, she puts out the welcome mat for God's Spirit to come and live in her temple. Therefore, to preoccupy yourself solely with what the exterior of the temple looks like (as the magazines suggest) and not to be concerned about the interior of the temple is not to understand God at all! Remember: "The LORD does not see as mortals see; they look on the outward appearance, but the LORD looks on the heart" (1 Samuel 16:7b, NRSV).

God wanted you to look like all of the families to whom you are related, whom God has blessed down through the ages. Never ever allow yourself or anyone else to lead you to believe that God made a series of errors when creating you. Remember that God was *working* when he created human beings. God our Creator was not at play! Never ever try to become someone else's definition of physical beauty by doing damage and bodily harm to yourself. It demonstrates ingratitude to God. It diminishes God's size, power, and plan for your life by implying that the divine plan is merely about your physical size, your shape, and your looks. That's wrong and God really hates it! Besides, do you really believe God is that superficial?

If you glance through God's Word, you will find that there aren't a lot of physical descriptions of people within those pages. Quite often broad adjectives are used to describe people like Goliath, who was more than nine feet tall (1 Samuel 17:4), or Samson's strength (Judges 15:14-15); others might have been described simply as "handsome" or "beautiful." Makes you wonder why Scripture would leave out details about a person's physical features, doesn't it? After all, was Mary, the mother of Christ, a size two, twelve, or twenty-two? What about Eve? What was her bra size? And, how about the hips of Sarah, Abraham's wife? How wide were they?

No, by omitting such details, God tells us that striving for physical, outward beauty ain't never scored points with him. Remember: God's the one who put you, and the rest of us, together. God's Word tells us in Proverbs 30:31, "charm is deceptive and beauty is fleeting" (NIV). To spend time sitting down inspecting your physical flaws is to look God in the eye and tell the Creator how to do his business. And, since you weren't around for God to consult during the creation of this world, I would think it's a little late to start now.

God makes no mistakes. All of the body parts and proportions you were born with were given to you with love and tender care. That includes your hair and the color of your skin! Such diversity was God's way of making you unique and special—so he could recognize you! Think about that when you and your friends get together. Look at the full and glorious range of God's color palette. Even the hairs on your own head are different colors!

You are in the body—the beautiful body and skin—the temple that God gave you. And since God gives you one temple only, you are required to take care if it—the interior (your heart and spirit) as well as the exterior!

So, my darlin', learn to do just that: To love, respect, honor, and take pride in your temple. Turn that stuff from the media off (especially that raunchy music on TV and the radio!) and get enough sleep. Learn to exercise your body. Learn how to keep a healthy and balanced diet. Drink lots of water. Keep your body clean. Keep your surroundings (like your room!) neat and clean for your own sense of order and peace. (You need to think in there!) Learn how to properly care for and pamper your skin, hair, and nails. Be mindful of what you put in your body that harms it physically (including cigarettes, alcohol, drugs, and junk food).

Rise early (yes, early) and appreciate the dawn of each and every new day, first by thanking God in prayer and reading his Word. Praise God for thinking enough of you to choose (yes, choose) you to see another day, another week, another year. Breathe long and deeply the air that God has provided. Be quiet, attentive, and *awake* in your classes at school. Be respectful of authority, of your parents and your elders, and of your peers, for they have much to teach you. Practice self-respect and self-control. Take time for yourself to think and reflect about yourself, your world, and your place within it.

Walk in the sun, run through the rain, and play in the snow. Rejoice and be thankful for God's goodness, grace, and mercy to you as you pull yourself up to the table that the Lord has provided. Thank God for the movement of your limbs and brain matter, for laughter and tears.

Show care and concern for the things you put in your emotional, psychological, and spiritual temple by monitoring what you read, listen to, and absorb. Surround yourself with "what is true and good and right. Think about things that are pure and lovely, and dwell on the fine, good things in others. Think about all you can praise God for and be glad about" (Philippians 4:8, TLB). Avoid things that pollute your spirit (Matthew 15:19; Galatians 5:19-21), as well as the people who bring such pollution into your personal space.

Go to the library and begin to read good books on African American history and literature. Listen to all kinds of music. When given the opportunity, go to recitals, concerts, the ballet, the opera, art galleries, and museums. Take mental notes so that you can learn to recognize good things (as well as garbage!) when you see and hear them. Pay attention to how broad and sweeping God's creativity is in humans...how God's gifts and talents in us are not narrow and one-dimensional.

Ask God to show you your own creative talents, whether those be music, drawing, sewing, cooking (learn how to do that!), knitting, gardening, writing, acting—whatever! God has given you those things. The Spirit will reveal them to you if you ask. Value your talents and use them in service to others.

Develop pride and respect for your family. Thank God for them. Talk to members of your extended family, and try to track down your physical features through your family tree.

Choose to believe that God loves you and wants only the best for you.

And, thank God for those hips!

A Prayer for You

O God, our great Creator,

What an awesome and wondrous thing you have done. You have created a one-of-a-kind gift to the world, this young woman. You are her Father and she is your daughter. The world is in awe of how you have blessed her with intelligence, great looks, a wonderful personality, and a curiosity about the things of you and this world.

Father, I pray for her right now. I ask for protection, security, and blessings for her. Open her eyes to the fact that when you created her you were *working* and not just "messing around." Plant in her spirit the fact that you don't make junk, only "good stuff," and that she is now and will forever be "good stuff." And, she will become even greater "stuff" as she grows in her wisdom and acceptance of you in her life and in her living. Bless her much, pick her up when she stumbles, and keep her in your care. In Christ's name, I pray. Amen.

For Your Consideration

1. What is your favorite physical feature on your body? Which family member shares the same feature?
2. List five talents that you know you possess. List five talents that people have told you you have. Are they the same?
3. Read Matthew 15:19 and Galatians 5:19-21. Describe "spiritual pollution." How does it affect you?

A Prayer from You

■ ■ ■

2

TRUTH

TO KNOW THAT YOU KNOW THAT YOU KNOW

Jesus said, "If you hold to my teaching, you are really my disciples. Then you will know the truth, and the truth will set you free." (John 8:31-32, NIV)

What has been will be again, what has been done will be done again; there is nothing new under the sun. Is there anything of which one can say, "Look! This is something new!" It was here already, long ago; it was here before our time. (Ecclesiastes 1:9-10, NIV)

My Dear One,

The Book of Ecclesiastes cautions us "ain't nothing new under the sun!" *Nothing!* Everything that exists has been around a long time. Humans may recycle it, repackage it, reconstitute it, even resurrect it, but it's been here before. It's a fact that applies to everything—clothes, food, habits, tastes, styles, and philosophies.

Don't be fooled or misled. People have been arguing about the existence of God, the creation of the universe, the existence and identity of Jesus, and the pros and cons of religion for as long as humans have existed.

There is a lot of new "stuff" out there that people claim to believe, much of it questionable. Some of it exists to test what you believe; even more of it exists to test the strength of your beliefs. It is important for you to understand that. As you grow, move around, meet new and interesting people, read, discuss, think, and hear things, the need to expand your thoughts, to experiment, "dabble," and "taste" other things is normal. It is just as important that you are certain and secure about what you *do* know. Be careful not to be "blown here and there by every wind of teaching" (Ephesians 4:14, NIV). You've got to know that you know. You also have to test what you know.

Well, what is it exactly that you should know? As a Christian or a member of what fellow Christians call the household of faith, we believe and hold these things as basic truth:

God, our Creator, created human beings in the divine image, in God's own likeness. As Creator, God is a Spirit is all-knowing (omniscient); all-present (omnipresent); and all-powerful (omnipotent). God is our Heavenly Father, and as our Father, God provides, cares for, loves, and forgives us. God is love, spirit, and truth.

Jesus Christ is the Son of God and our Savior. He lived as a human, died a most tortured death, was buried, and was raised again for forgiveness of our sins. When we (humans) are born, we are born into sin. The Bible teaches that "without the shedding of blood there is no forgiveness of sin" (Hebrews 9:22, TLB), and Jesus shed that blood so we would not have to do so.

In order for human beings to receive the assurance of eternal life (meaning, life in heaven with God after death on earth), we must know and *accept* Jesus Christ as God's Son and our Savior. "Jesus said to him, 'I am the way, and the truth, and the life. No one comes to the Father except through me. If you know me, you will know my Father also'" (John 14:6-7, NRSV). By "confessing with your mouth, 'Jesus is Lord,' and believing in your heart that God raised him from the dead," you will be saved. "For it is with your heart that you believe and are justified [i.e., declared innocent], and it is with your mouth that you confess and are saved" (Romans 10:9-10, NIV).

As Christians, we understand that God does not call us to live a life of perfection but one of holiness. This means that the manner in which we live our lives—our actions, character, and attitude—should reflect the character, attitude, and actions of Christ (humility, patience, love, etc.). As we grow spiritually and develop a relationship with Christ, our goal and purpose is to become more like him. We begin to realize that this transformation happens only when we grow to rely less on ourselves and our intellect, abilities, and talents and more on God, the ultimate source of strength, power, and protection.

As humans we are born with an instinctive knowledge of God. (Remember your science classes at school, about instinct versus learned behavior?) "God has put this knowledge in their [our] hearts" (Romans 1:19, TLB). In other words, God places that—the internal knowledge that God does exist—inside our temple.

The Bible is the holy Word of God (given to humanity by God), and we accept and embrace its teaching—in its totality—as truth. As Christians, we believe that the Bible is the guide to peace, happiness, and liberation—the freedom from negativity in all forms (guilt, anger, fear, etc.).

We do not believe *in* Satan, but we do believe that Satan and demons exist—not as "people" but as a negative spiritual force that can only be dealt with by the spirit and power of God (Ephesians 6:12-13).

Even at your young age, God encourages you to ask, seek, and knock in order for you to get to know him. And, Jesus promised that "everyone who asks receives, and everyone who searches finds, and for everyone who knocks, the door will be opened" (Matthew 7:8, NRSV). God is a very big God who can handle any and everything you ask of him. If you ask God in sincerity to reveal himself to you and believe that the Lord has the power to do so, he will.

Your path to spiritual maturity will bend and twist; veer off to the left a little and sometimes lean to the right. But, as long as you know where "home base" is—as long as you "know that you know that you know" who God is and his importance in your life, you'll be OK.

Those of us who are watching you grow and question will brace ourselves for the "new" that you will attempt to introduce to us. We will smile thinking back on our own encounter with the "new," and we will pray.

A Prayer for You

God of All,

I thank you for young and budding "seedlings" of faith. I pray for nurturing...for good soil, much rain, and plentiful sunshine to help this tender seedling take root, grow, develop, and prosper in you. May she be like "one of the trees growing beside a stream, trees that produce fruit in season" (Psalm 1:3, CEV). Remind her, dear God, in those moments when the demons of doubt, fear, and loneliness attack her that when she calls you, you not only hear her but you answer her as well. Hold her close as she struggles to search for the answers, and guide her feet so they stay on the path that leads to you. Surround her with your angels of love, mercy, protection, and support. I ask this in Jesus' name. Amen.

For Your Consideration

1. Do you believe in God? Do you believe that God loves you? Why or why not?
2. Write a description of God. Include physical, character, and personality characteristics. Where does your description come from? How would God describe you?
3. Read Ephesians 6:12. What does this Scripture mean to you and your life?

A Prayer from You

. . .

3

GRATITUDE

STOP! THANK-YOU TIME!

Do not be anxious about anything, but in everything, by prayer and petition, with thanksgiving, present your requests to God. (Philippians 4:6, NIV)

My Dear One,

We live in a culture that teaches us that what we have is what we are. You and members of your generation feel it in all of the many things you are programmed to buy, want, have, use, drink, drive, and wear. The message is that you are nothing if you do not have certain material things. So, what does that mean for those who don't have those certain things? For those whose financial situations don't allow for those things?

My darlin', there are some very important lessons here that you can not afford to miss, so pay attention.

Lesson #1: This constant parade of you-must-have-or-you-are-nothing stuff teaches you *covetousness*, a word not used very often these days. But, it's a word that God tells us is a no-no. (Check out the tenth commandment: "You shall

15

not covet your neighbor's house. You shall not covet your neighbor's wife, or his manservant of maidservant, his ox or donkey, or anything that belongs to your neighbor" (Exodus 20:17, NIV).

Webster's Dictionary defines covetousness as "an inordinate [meaning, over the top] desire for material possessions; of the possessions of others." By now you are probably arguing that that's not you, but think about it; it is.

When you think of the constant barrage from the media—the magazines, the "fashion police," television, music videos, etc.—isn't it just one long never-ending stream of buy-this, get-that, want-this, must-have-that messages? Be cool, hip, popular, "down," or "in" by having _____ (you can fill in the blank). It leads you into wanting what you don't have (or need), always checking out what's new that others have, and questioning why you don't or can't have the same things. It keeps you constantly searching for the next new thing, the next must-have. You see it at school. Hardly a day goes by without someone showing off the "new thing" of the moment.

My darlin', this brings us to the second lesson: *ingratitude*.

Lesson #2: This constant desire to have creates dissatisfaction, envy, and greed, but most important, it gives birth to ingratitude. And, that's not good. And yes, young people aren't the only ones who suffer from this disease; adults do, too. Back in the day it was called "keeping up with the Joneses." The days haven't changed. Old school or new school, all of us must learn to appreciate all that we have been blessed to possess.

Covetousness teaches us ingratitude by tempting us to ignore the simple things in life, to focus on those things that can be bought, sold, and traded, to pursue those things that are temporary. (Hello, Satan!) It totally dismisses and devalues those things that money cannot buy...the things of God, such as love, self-respect, honor, good health, strength, your family, your friends, birds, sunshine, rain, grace, forgiveness, and mercy. Those things are eternal, invaluable, precious, and free to all. They are the things for which we must demonstrate gratitude and learn to thank God for on a daily basis.

Lesson #3: This covetousness stuff is time-consuming and just plain exhausting! Declare defeat now and don't even get in the rat's maze of trying to compete or keep up. You can't! Stop looking at others and pining, whining, and stressing over what they have and what you don't.

There is an old hymn of the church that speaks of counting our blessings. In fact the words to the old hymn by J. Oatman and E. Excell encourage us to "count your blessings, name them one by one." The next time you get the urge to check out what's new and question why you don't have it, think about that song and just whisper a prayer of gratitude for all that you *do* have.

A Prayer for You

O God, the Source of all things,

Oh, how the world sings a never-ending song of "want that," "be this," and "have the other." Sometimes it can be overwhelming. So Lord, I pray that in those times when the noises of the world sing that old song that you would send up a new song in your daughter's spirit. Let it be a song of how much you love her, care for her, provide for her, and protect her. Remind her of all that she is blessed to have. Open her eyes, her heart, and her spirit that she not be too quick to miss the sound of the wind, the green of the grass, and the warmth of sunshine on her face. Let her feel your presence in all that she does. Let her see you and know the blessing of having you in her life. Keep her mindful of the fact that since you are her Father, she has everything that she will ever need. In Jesus' name, I ask these things, knowing that you have promised it. Amen.

For Your Consideration

1. Name the following:
   - The "new" thing that everyone is wearing at school
   - The singer/group that everyone is listening to
   - The "new" thing that everyone is talking about
2. Define "everyone." What was "everyone" wearing, listening to, and wanting last year?
3. Read Numbers 15:34. Look up the word *lust* in the dictionary. What does this word teach us about desire?

A Prayer from You

. . .

4

FAITH

GO, DARLIN'! GO, DARLIN'! KEEP YOUR HEAD UP! KEEP YOUR HEAD UP!

I was young and now I am old, yet I have never seen the righteous forsaken or their children begging bread. (Psalm 37:25, NIV)

God will meet all your needs according to his glorious riches in Christ Jesus. (Philippians 4:19, NIV)

My Dear One,

If you took a minute to look through the business and entertainment sections of the daily newspaper, you might come away with the impression that economically all is well and everyone who has the desire is making all kinds of money (celebrities, rappers, athletes, pop-stars, etc.). However, if you were to read those sections more closely, you would find that thousands of people are losing their jobs every day. For every person who experiences a job loss, the impact can be devastating and is felt directly by the family of that person. Perhaps this has happened to you and your family, a relative, or a friend. It makes for difficult, stressful, and often scary times.

God promises—yes, promises—a lot about these kinds of hard times. The Lord assures us "never will I leave you; never will I forsake you" (Hebrews 13:5, NIV); God "will meet all your needs according to his glorious riches in Christ Jesus" (Philippians 4:19, NIV), and that because "the LORD is my shepherd, I shall not want" (Psalm 23:1, KJV).

If you and your family are presently going through hard times (unemployment, the loss of a home, divorce, incarceration, etc.), hold on. Don't give up hope. Stay faithful. As difficult as it might be, try to stand back and look at your situation in a different way. Try to think of your experiences as a kind of history for you and your family, a "Family History of God's Grace."

As you move through this, try to pay attention to those things that you pray about and ask God for—those things you need but can't figure out how they will be obtained. Watch your parents and other family members. If everyone else is too overwhelmed, hurt, angry, and confused to pray, then *you* pray. Yes, God is more than aware of your situation. (God is omniscient—all-knowing—remember?) But most of the time, God wants to hear us call his name with our own voices. God wants us to ask him to provide all that we need. God wants us to ask so he can supply, and then we can thank God for what only he has done for us. The Bible says "do not be anxious about anything [meaning, don't worry], but in everything, by prayer and petition, with thanksgiving, present your requests to God" (Philippians 4:6, NIV). Then, trust and have faith in the Lord that he will do all that we ask, in God's own way and in his own time.

When all of that happens, that divine intervention becomes a permanent part of your "Family History of God's Grace." As you and your family grow to live as God would have you live, trusting in the Lord and staying strong in his Word, you are adding more and more pages to this history.

As you get older, grow up, and begin your adult life, you may find yourself experiencing some of these same kinds of setbacks. That will be the time to draw from the memory bank of your family history. You will be able to recall the fear, apprehension, stress, and tension brought about by past problems and trials, but you will also be able to remember praying to God, trusting him, reading the Word, staying faithful, and watching God resolve those problems. Those memories will teach you to repeat that same process. And hopefully, the memories will begin to teach you to do two more things.

First, in remembering how wonderful it felt to have God meet your needs in hard times, you will want that feeling to continue in good times as well. So, no matter your condition or situation, in good or bad times, you will always call on God. In the same way that God is there to help you in the tough times, God is more than ready to sustain you in the good as well.

The apostle Paul in his letter to the Philippian church said, "I've been up and I've been down. I've had a lot, and days when I was really in need, but through all of it, no matter what, I've learned to be at peace. Christ Jesus will give me the strength to face everything that I need to face" (Philippians 4:12-14, TLB). Think about that for a minute. That's a pretty powerful statement.

Second, recalling God's faithfulness through the years should teach you to offer an act of thanksgiving for all that God has brought you through and blessed you to have. In considering all God has given to you, you should learn to return a portion of it to God. I'm talking about tithing.

Despite the fact that the Bible speaks of tithing (see Malachi 3:10), some adult Christians (who may not have grown up spiritually...it's a process, darlin') say that tithing is a hard concept to master. Not so. If you begin in your youth, as you grow, you begin to understand how simple it really is and the importance of having it as a part of your life. Tithing is an act of faith, of thanksgiving, and of making a statement to God that, no matter what, you are putting him first!

If you look through the Old Testament, you will find all kinds of offerings that people gave as a statement to the Lord (sacrifices of animals, oil, flour, etc.). For us, tithing is simply the act of returning to God a tenth (10 cents out of every dollar) of our earnings. This tithe is given first, before we figure out who else needs to be paid. It is also given with the understanding that anything and everything else that we might need we trust God to supply. That, my darlin', is called faith.

As a young person, you would tithe a tenth of your allowance or any money that you might earn through part-time jobs (babysitting, etc.). You might also choose to tithe on any monetary gifts (Christmas, birthdays, etc.) that you might receive.

Another thing you must understand is that when we tithe, we present it to God in the church. Our tithes are used to maintain our churches, to pay the salaries of staff, and to make contributions toward helping the poor and missionaries in foreign countries. Our financial giving is not limited to the tithe, but begins with the tithe. The next lesson is to give it happily and not with an attitude. God does not *need* our tithe; he *wants* it.

We also tithe with our time and talents. That can mean any kind of service in God's house (ushering, singing, dance or drama ministries, etc.) as well as serving in the community or world (tutoring, going on mission trips, volunteering in shelters, soup kitchens, nursing homes, or hospitals, etc.).

Again, this tithe of time, talents, and money is a way of thanking God for all the pages in your "Family History of God's Grace" and a way to pass on the blessing of his provision to you and your family to others. (Did you see that movie *Pay It Forward*?) It is a way of saying that hard times may be here for awhile, but they do not last forever. Tithing is also an act that will bring you much joy, happiness, and a ton of blessings—that's the floodgates described in Malachi 3:10.

And your faithfulness in this, my darlin', makes God so proud that he puts your picture on the heavenly refrigerator!

A Prayer for You

Jehovah Jireh, God of provision,

As your children, we are so happy that you know all things…when we will have good times as well as not-so-good times. How grateful we are that you have promised us that no matter what the circumstances, you, your love, and your provision for us will be there, always.

I call on you right now, Lord, that when the not-so-good times, the hard times, come to your daughter or to her family, you will remind her of your presence, listening and already working things out for her, and their, good. Strengthen her that she might not lose faith, hope, or sight of you. Reassure her that you will provide because you know what is needed. Keep her focused, calm, and at peace with you. Teach her that fresh pages in her "Family History of God's Grace" are there to make her strong for future days and times.

Give her patience to understand and accept that her time for movement may not be your time, but when you do move, it will always be the right time. Bless her with a sense of humor despite less-than-humorous circumstances. Remind her that the songs of our ancestors are true: Weeping may endure for a night, but joy comes in the morning! In Jesus' name, I pray. Amen.

For Your Consideration

1. Describe a difficult situation that you or your family has experienced (or are currently experiencing). How was it resolved? How did God reveal himself in it?
2. Read Malachi 3:8-10. What is a tithe? What is your tithe?

A Prayer from You

■ ■ ■

5

HOLD ON—TIGHT!

"For I know the plans I have for you," declares the LORD,... *"plans to give you hope and a future."* *(Jeremiah 29:11,* NIV*)*

All the days ordained for me were written in your book before one of them came to be. (Psalm 139:15, NIV*)*

My Dear One,

As you are growing up, you probably hear folks tell you, "These days are the happiest days of your life!", "Enjoy these days!", "Don't grow up too fast!", and "Since you are so young you don't have any responsibilities." But, for too many teenagers, these words are not true. These days are not their happiest days, and many have no choice but to grow up quickly in order to take on the responsibilities that have been placed on them. Some teens are growing up in the chaos and confusion of divorce and domestic upheaval. Others face parental job loss and constant movement for shelter and a real place to call home. Some grapple with the pain of losing a parent to drug addiction, alcoholism, emotional depression, incarceration, and the lifestyles that accompany these things. Still others may be caught up in the foster-care system, and no two days are ever the same; families, schools, houses are always changing. For many teens, cancer, AIDS, and other kinds of illnesses have robbed them of parents. And there are teens who are being raised by grandparents and great-grandparents who have already raised one set of children during their younger years. Now age has sapped them of energy, health, and strength as they try to be there to raise and love this new set of teens. Or, maybe the parents have traded an active and involved presence in the life of their teen for work. How many parents try to convince themselves that as long as the child has the latest, the best, the most expensive new thing out there, he or she will be happy, content, and convinced of Mom or Dad's love?

These are difficult times for so many of our youth—perhaps even for you.

Oh, how much we as parents have messed this up. How we have allowed our own temples to become corroded and polluted with materialism and our immaturity and selfishness. We cannot begin to find the words for an apology that would begin to heal all of the hurts we have caused.

Would the words "I'm sorry" sound like a foreign language to you?

Despite all of this however, there are a few things that you must know.

First, the hurt, pain, disappointment, and anger are real, and you have the right to feel those emotions. Too many adults have failed miserably at being parents, and our excuses are many. For far too many of us, our lives are the direct result of the choices and decisions that we have made—totally depending on our own thoughts, intellect, and smarts—choices and decisions that are (sometimes) reparable, but for whatever reasons, we have not yet chosen to change and make the necessary repairs.

My dear one, please know this: One day, all of us, every single person on the face of the earth, must stand before God and give an accounting of all that we have done. No one gets away with anything. God will hold us responsible for all of our actions. Yes, the Lord is merciful, but we will still bear the consequences for the things that we have—and have not—done.

Second, do not give up hope. Choose to believe that God does see and know all things…that what you are presently experiencing God is using to mold, shape, and direct your life. And that God loves you and has only the best in store for you.

Third, pray for your parents and those who assume responsibility for you, that God will become their choice. Don't dismiss or ignore the support and love God sends to you simply because it doesn't look like you want it to look. The kids at school you are beating up; the teacher that you cuss out much too often; the principal you think is stupid; the grandparent you see as just too old; or that foster parent who gets on your last nerve…all of them are really trying to teach you something. They are probably the very people that God is sending to love you. The real deal, darlin'? The number of people that you can beat up, cuss out, or be rude and ugly to does not determine your strength. It is the number of people whom you can love in the midst of chaos that truly determines just how strong you are.

And finally, never, ever think that no one hears you. God is always listening and always moving. God's Word promises us that "he neither slumbers, nor sleeps.... The LORD watches over you.... The LORD will watch over your life" (Psalm 121:4-7, NIV).

Choose to believe that God has big plans for you and your life...that all of your days, even these hard days, are in the divine plans for you...and that in the end, you will know victory, peace, and joy.

Just hold on—tight!

A Prayer for You

Father God,

I lift this child and her situation up to you. I know that you know her because you were there shaping and forming her in her mother's womb. Before her mother ever felt her move and kick, you knew her. You were there at her birth and have been with her every day of her life—even in times when she felt that she was alone.

I ask now, Lord, that you hold her even closer so that in the painful times, the hurtful times, the times that she would strike back at the world and those around her, in those times, she will feel something inside that she can only explain as being you.

Remind her, Lord, that you do not forsake for she is much too precious to you. You are peace of mind, body, and spirit. Provide her with all that she can hold. Remove the pain, the anger, the loneliness, and the willingness to hurt others, and replace it with the desire to show and know love. Let her see you, Lord. Let her know in her heart that you are indeed her Father in heaven, and above all earthly fathers and mothers with all of our faults and short-comings. And, as her Father, you will not fail. In Jesus' name, I pray and ask it all. Amen.

For Your Consideration

1. What do you cry about? What are you doing to cope with it?
2. Apologize to three people whom you have hurt. Name five people you need to pray for. Pray for them now.
3. Read Psalm 5. What consolation does it give?

A Prayer from You

■ ■ ■

6

LOVE

YOUR TEMPLE'S SECURITY AND ALARM SYSTEM

Love is patient, love is kind. It does not envy, it does not boast, it is not proud. It is not rude, it is not self-seeking, it is not easily angered; it keeps no record of wrongs. Love does not delight in evil but rejoices with the truth. It always protects, always trusts, always hopes, always perseveres. (1 Corinthians 13:4-7, NIV)

My Dear One,

The media, the cosmetics industry, the fashion police—in other words, the "world" has created a definition of *love*. They define it as being fragile, temporary, vulnerable, unpredictable, and unreliable. But here's the real deal on that: God's Word teaches us that *God* is love; therefore, love is strong, resilient, and does not change. And there is nothing fragile, temporary, vulnerable, unpredictable, or unreliable about that!

In 1 Corinthians 13, the apostle Paul gives a working definition of love—or what I like to call "The Whistles-Bells-and-Flashing-Lights Love Security and Alarm System" for your temple. That's right, your temple is so precious to God that a security and alarm system was specially created for it. (What? Do you think that a building or a car, with its alarm system, is more precious than you? Girl, puhleeze!) As your understanding of love deepens and matures according to the scriptural definition, the alarm system becomes "activated."

My darlin', pay attention.

Paul begins by stating not only what love *is* but more importantly, what love is *not*. He says that love is patient, meaning that it requires time (as in building a relationship), and it is kind. But then he says that love is "never jealous, boastful, proud, or rude. Love isn't selfish or quick-tempered. It doesn't keep a record of wrongs that others do. Love rejoices in the truth, but not in evil. Love is always supportive, loyal, hopeful, and trusting. Love never fails" (CEV).

So, what does this mean to you and your peers?

Well, for one thing, it really blows a hole in most of the stuff that a lot of songs, raps, movies, videos, TV shows, and soap operas claim: Love is *not* a game. It is not only a noun; it is also a verb. And it is not a feeling that comes and goes based on who you are looking at in any given moment. It is too important to be treated in such a casual and careless way. Since God is love, he takes the matter of love very seriously.

Check out what is happening in the hallways at school or on the sidewalks. Do you ever see scenes like the following?

A small group of guys are standing around (in the hall, by a car, near a locker, etc.) and talking about who has the most "control" over women. One of the guys may see a girl passing (perhaps his girlfriend), call to her, and rudely demand that she come to him—immediately. On one hand, you could look at it as him being playful and showing off in front of his friends, a pretty harmless act. On the other hand, it is rude, boastful, and embarrassing for the young woman. It is not cool or hip or "showin' respect." It is disrespectful. Remember: it works both ways; girls do the same thing and it is still wrong. (Do you hear anything?)

Or, let's say you meet a young man at school who you think is pretty nice. You talk on the phone a lot, and you think he could be special. As the relationship begins to develop, you begin to notice that he questions you about your activities at school or church. (You *are* actively involved, right?) When you have choir rehearsal, he wants to take you to a movie. When you need to study, he wants to keep you on the phone. When you have meetings or services at church, he wants to know why you can't do other things with him. If you invite him to come to church with you, he refuses, has a million excuses, or cops an attitude. After awhile, you begin to feel that you are being asked to choose between paying attention to him or fulfilling your duties and obligations at home, at church, at school, etc. He says that he really cares for you, perhaps even loves you. You like him, too, but you don't like the pressure.

Now that pressure you are feeling, my darlin'? Here's the real deal on that: It's your alarm system going off! Pay attention to it, and don't ignore it or try to turn it off by making excuses for him. You know that "head" talk? "Maybe he's nervous around people at church"; "I can study later; I'm doing okay in that class"; "Maybe I'm crazy, he's not that bad." Yeah, that talk! You're not crazy, stupid, or nuts. You feel the pressure because it *is* pressure. This is jealousy, and love is never jealous.

The story is told of a young lady who was in a relationship with an up-and-coming professional football player. His incredible salary afforded him the means to shower her with lovely and lavish gifts that she very happily accepted. She thought she had hit the "lottery jackpot" of love. A few months into the relationship, he presented her with a cell phone, "just to stay in touch." As it turned out, he tried to "stay in touch" by demanding to know her movements 24/7. He bragged to his friends and fellow teammates that he was in love; and that she belonged to him. She complained to her friends that she was beginning to realize (i.e., her alarm system was going off!) that he was jealous, possessive, and controlling. She also questioned how she could end the relationship.

Looking at the definition of love in the Scriptures, do you see love in those scenarios?

As God's people, we are taught to give our love to others from a loving, giving heart and a generous spirit. There is nothing there, however, that says we are to be stupid and foolish about it. The love alarm system works in combination with your heart and mind. Listen to the whistles, bells, and flashing lights going off before your eyes, because the alarm goes off in your head when you are hearing, seeing, and feeling things that are the direct opposite of what God's Word says about love. It keeps you safe and out of harm's way. (Satan's busy, honey.) It protects you when people try to suck you into that destructive, manipulative head trip called "if-you-love-me-then-you-will-_____" (fill in the blank). The alarm system tells you to stay away from that because it is not of God.

Think about it for a moment. How many unwanted, unplanned, "it-was-a-mistake" babies have been born, drugs taken, alcohol consumed, lies told, crimes committed, and lives lost and destroyed—all because of people trying to fill in that blank? Or, consider the vast numbers of women, young and not-so-young, involved in relationships where there is domestic violence and physical, mental, and emotional abuse. Or the overwhelming numbers of females in prisons as a direct result of trying to prove their love by filling in that blank. To all of that damage, hurt, anguish, and pain, 1 Corinthians 13 says, Ain't none of that love!

Do not allow this to happen to you! Don't allow Satan to bend, twist, and distort God's concept of love in order to satisfy his desire to have you bound and gagged in sin, feeling like there is no way out! Don't get caught up in receiving "gifts" that aren't gifts at all but are a noose around your neck. Don't allow your sense of who and what you are—God's child—to be destroyed (Matthew 7:6).

God did not create you to be a punching bag (physical or verbal) for anybody! Darlin', this is no mere whistle, bell, or flashing light going off; this is a siren wailing in your ear! *Move!* Walk—no, *run* away from an abusive relationship as fast as you can! Want the real deal? Regardless of how cute, fine, sweet, apologetic, generous, and hip he is, kick that boy to the curb if he starts up with that "if-you-love-me" lame and sorry song!

Listen and heed the warnings (Matthew 11:15). Learn what the Word of God says about love. Choose to believe it, embrace it, and live by it. Let God do the man/boyfriend/husband selection. God wants only the best for you. So, trust the Lord to present his choice at the right time in your life.

Finally, look around and pay attention. Begin to observe what love really is and what it looks like—among your family, between couples, old and young, who you know are struggling to apply God's love in their marriages. Even look among you and your friends! You will begin to understand that love is indeed a wondrous thing. It can make you cry sometimes (OK, not all of the songs are wrong), but true love will build two people up to be the very best that God would have them be. True love supports a positive sense of self-esteem. And true love, in its patience and kindness, waits.

And that, my darlin', keeps the whistles, bells, and flashing lights from going off!

A Prayer for You

God of Love,

How different your definition of love is from the world's. How positive, giving, caring, protective, and loving is your definition. O God, we are your children; we love you and the way that you love us.

So, God, I pray now for your daughter in her questioning and searching for love. As she moves through the push-and-pull, tug-and-tear of the world, keep her anchored in your love and care. Keep her heart and mind. Help her to turn a deaf ear to those forces that would cause her to question and doubt your love and care for her.

Teach her first how to love you, to love herself, and then to love others. Reassure her that you know her and her needs. Teach her to bring everything, every little part of herself to you, withholding nothing so that you can mold and shape her into the loving person you want her to be. Show her love in the people around her, in her own actions, and in the little things of life that you have created. Forgive her, Lord, when she would be less than loving. Give her a repentant heart and spirit for those times, and then point her in the right direction.

Give her patience so that she will not move in her own mind but in your Spirit, in your time. Teach her to look to you always in matters of the heart, spirit, and everything else that impacts her life. I pray this to you for this child, for her life. In Jesus' name, I ask. Amen.

For Your Consideration

1. Read Matthew 7:6. How does this apply to you and your peers?
2. What is your definition of *love?* Write a love song.

A Prayer from You

• • •

PART TWO

THE REAL DEAL

ON CONSTRUCTING YOUR TEMPLE

7

FRIENDSHIP

ONE OR TWO REAL ONES WILL DO JUST FINE

A friend loves at all times. (Proverbs 17:17, NIV)

My Dear One,

As we grow and develop, friends become very important to us. In many ways, they help influence, mold, and shape us into the people we eventually become. We can learn so much about God and ourselves from our friends. That is why it is so very important that we seek God's guidance and direction in choosing our friends.

When God promises not to leave nor forsake us, many times that vow is fulfilled through the love and concern that our friends show us…in the ways that they stick with us through good and bad times. Sometimes we see it in the ways that friends appear during times of sickness, or after the death of a loved one. We look up or turn around and they are there with open arms and strong shoulders to lean on, ready to dry our tears. Sometimes we see it in the ways our friends sense how we feel, what we need, and what we want—just by our facial expressions, our body language, or our silence. Sometimes our friends are there to supply financial or material needs that we may never have expressed out loud—except in prayer to God. Too often we see such friendship as being purely circumstantial, but it isn't. Such friends are the presence of God in our lives when we need that presence most.

Friends also teach us a lot about ourselves. True friends are not easy with us but are frank and honest. Often, they have a way of holding up a mirror to us, letting us know our weaknesses, faults, insecurities, selfishness, smallness, and when we are downright "perpetratin'"! These things are not always easy to hear, but friendship opens our ears and our hearts.

True friends push and challenge us to be better people than we ever believed we could be. They help us do our very best. Think about the times in school when your friends really get on your case because you don't speak up for yourself or because you fail to give the answers in class—knowing that you have them and that they are correct! How many times have your friends "dogged" you for not demonstrating how smart, talented, or athletic you really are? How many times have they pushed you forward to volunteer to do something because they knew you could do whatever there was to be done and that you would do a great job? How many times have they angered you because they knew that you were going the wrong way and they forced you to stop and seek advice from an adult? In how many ways, my darlin', has God placed people—friends—in your path to lead you, encourage you, and bless you?

Conversely, how many people do you associate with and call "friend" who are not friends at all? How many of them have you sought out because of who they were in your social group, for who they knew, or because of what they had? How many have chosen you as a friend for all of those same reasons? In other words, how many "friends" of yours have been unwisely chosen, without God doing the leading and guiding? Think about that for a minute, and keep those thoughts in mind. Stay tuned: this is discussed more later in this book (see chapter 14, "Negativity").

Friendship is important—so important that even God had a friend. His name was Abraham (James 2:23). And, we can't forget that Jesus had Peter, James, and John (who was described as "the disciple Jesus loved") as his best friends.

In Proverbs 17:17, it says "a friend loves at all times." How wonderful it is to know that God sends friends to us to love us even though, at times, we are not very lovable or fun to be around.

My darlin', thank God every day for your friends and for the ways they help you build your temple. Pray for them and their families. Ask God to lead and guide them to become the people that he wants them to be, the same way God wants to lead and guide you. Thank God for sending them to you, and ask the Holy Spirit to help you become the friend that your friends need.

A Prayer for You

Father God,

What a blessing it is to have friends; to have people in our lives that stand by us, support us, and represent you. Thank you for them.

I pray for your daughter and for the friends you have placed in her life. Guide her and direct her in choosing good friends...true friends. Let them speak your words of care and concern to her. Give her an open heart and listening ears when they try to help her, and keep her out of harm's way. Teach her to count true friends as part of the treasure that you have for her life.

Keep this child and her friends in your care and protection, and lead all of them to become the people that you would have them become. What a wonderful way to show your love to us—in the gift of a good friend! In Jesus' name, I pray. Amen.

For Your Consideration

1. Make a list of your closest friends. Why are they your friends?
2. Review your list. Is there anyone who should *not* be on that list? Think a moment. Is there anyone who should be *added* to the list?
3. Read Luke 5:1-11. How does Jesus meet his first friends?

A Prayer from You

■ ■ ■

8

KNOWLEDGE

ANSWERS TO THE "WHY" QUESTIONS OF LIFE

...knowledge with good sense will lead you to life. (Ecclesiastes 7:12b, CEV)

The fear of the LORD is the beginning of knowledge, but fools despise wisdom and discipline. (Proverbs 1:7, NIV)

My Dear One,

As parents, many of us (the Baby Boomers of the late 1940s and early '50s) were raised by a generation of people who worked hard, struggled to provide for us, loved us in their own way, and tried to give us spiritual roots. One of the main tenets of our parents' generation was the absolute importance of education for young black people. For the most part, as children we were told to "seek ye first...an education"! And as children we generally obeyed. Many of us went to college; we got that education, that degree.

The "seek ye first" part was a paraphrasing of a Scripture passage (Matthew 6:33). In many ways it was a mistake for that passage to be used in that way because it gave us the distorted impression that education would lead to everything we would ever need.

Our lives as adults reflect the limitations of that original advice from our parents. Many of us have degrees and diplomas up the "wazoo," but those achievements have not helped. Current statistics on adult alcoholism, drug use (both recreational and prescription), credit card indebtedness, and divorce rates clearly demonstrate that our "educated" souls and spirits know no peace and little joy.

The recent trend of companies "downsizing" and laying off great numbers of workers (many of whom are parents of dependent children) has shown us the fallacy of placing so much of our faith in degrees, jobs, careers, cars, homes, and other forms of material security. (Remember that chapter on covetousness? Yeah, adults are guilty of it, too.) Experience has also shown how our focus on things of the world has taken our attention from things of God, things such as you, our children. We owe you and God an apology, from the very depths of our souls.

My darlin', when you seek God first, you find the purpose to which God has called you. You don't worry about how many cars you will own or how much money you'll make. When you attend college, you don't go looking at the careers that claim to pay the most or those that receive the most acclaim. You seek out the career and the life work that you know within yourself honors God first, challenges your skills, and yields peace, joy, happiness, and fulfillment in your life. With everything entrusted to God, you stay faithful, knowing that the Lord will lead you to the financial support that will be needed in order for you to do his work.

When you seek God first, you have no need to go through life asking "Who am I?" or "Why am I here?" You know why you are here—to do the work that God calls you to do and to use the talents, skills, and intelligence the Lord has given to you. You become a fellow worker in God's vineyard. You take care of the earth and its natural resources, as well as the people who live on it. You take care of yourself—your mind and body—so you are always ready to go where God leads you, ever ready to serve. That means not polluting your body and mind with drugs, alcohol, or other things that are stupid and foolish. It means keeping yourself whole, abstaining from sex until God presents you with marriage to the mate he has selected for you. You become available to God.

All that being said, seeking God first *also* means educating yourself to be the best you can be, so that God can send you out as a light to the world. It means staying attentive and productive in your classes. How will you know exactly where God wants you to be if you are absent, asleep, bored, rude to your teachers, and generally not there? How can God develop your skills if you are afraid to try new and challenging subjects such as math and science? (Come on, my darlin', folks are sick out there! We need cures for diseases!) How can God open new doors of educational opportunities for you if you are afraid that you won't get a boyfriend if the guys think you are smart? How can God grow you up to be that competent professional if you hold back, sit on, and generally stifle your creativity? How does God make this world better for all of us if you take the position that reaching higher, reading more, speaking clearly and correctly is something for white people and only white people? (Call that negative peer pressure!)

What a slap in God's face to have him enrich your life with such precious gifts—your wonderful, active mind, your talent, your creativity, your skills and abilities—and you, by not using them, tell God that he is wrong to give them to you. Oh, my darlin', don't do that. Don't even think about doing that! Don't make Satan happy so easily.

Darlin', I truly believe that when we are born, God stamps our future professions and occupations on our foreheads. It is only when asking God while standing in the light of his Word and his love that the Spirit will reveal that which God has written. Don't let anybody fool you: God and God alone knows the plans that he has for you (Jeremiah 29:11). It doesn't matter if your friends or family think it's valuable work or not. The work God calls all of us to do is precious in his sight—honorable, needed, and custom-made for our individual selves, talents, and skills. That must be what we value.

During my years of working as an academic advisor for colleges and universities, I would often ask my students the question, "What kind of person do you want to be?" The overwhelming majority would answer, "A very rich person!" Others could not answer the question at all because they had never thought about it. And, there were still others who felt that the pressures on them were so great, it was not important what kind of person *they* wanted to be; they had to become the person that *others* expected them to be.

Seek God first in your life, trusting and believing that he has set aside a work for you that no one else can claim. Stay vigilant and alert to those who help you along the way. They are preparing you for the work. Honor, respect, and pay attention to your teachers. Appreciate all that they do (the fussing, pushing, and pulling) as well as the things they don't do (like making things too easy for you) in order to help you become the best that you can be.

Begin to talk to members of your family or church, your friends, your neighbors, and other professionals about the kinds of work that they do. Ask them how they feel about their work, if they are happy doing it and why. Ask them if it is the work that God has called them to do. Listen closely to their answers. Attend church prayer meetings sometimes and listen to the testimonies of those in attendance. You will hear stories of how God provided even when jobs paid little, how children were educated on the strength of prayers, as well as how God uses his power to create opportunities where none appear to exist.

In the Old Testament book of 2 Chronicles 1:7-12, Solomon prays to God for help with his new job—being king. He didn't have a clue as to what to expect or if he could live up to all that was expected of him. He was scared and unsure of himself. So he prayed to God for wisdom in all things. He pledged that if God would help him, he would obey God and do all that the Lord wanted him to do. God heard Solomon and blessed him with great wisdom. In fact, there has never been another human being with the wisdom of King Solomon. Incidentally, God also made him the richest man on earth!

"But seek ye first his kingdom and his righteousness, and all these things will be given to you as well" (Matthew 6:33, KJV).

A Prayer for You

Our Father who art in heaven,
I know that you have placed within this child a longing

to do the work that you have "stamped" on her forehead, placed in her spirit, and assigned to her hands. Place her in the light of your Word, so that you can show her how to prepare herself for the work. Prepare her temple, Lord. Give her strength, courage, and endurance when she would appear weak and overwhelmed. Hold her tongue when she would speak at the times that you need her to be quiet and listening. Place in her path the people who will lead her to the place that you and only you have set aside for her.

Let her not grow weary or impatient; jealous or confused by the pace of others. Keep her mindful that all you have set aside for her is for her and her alone; no one else can claim it. Give her joy as she learns new and challenging things about this world you have created. Give her sweet peace at night so she can wake up excited and interested in school, her teachers, and her future. In Jesus' name, I pray. Amen.

For Your Consideration

1. What kind of person do you want to be? What kinds of things are you seeking in life?
2. List three careers you think you would like to pursue. Talk to two people working in each of those careers. Ask them these questions: Are you happy doing this? Do you believe that this is what God has called you to do?
3. Read Ecclesiastes 2:17-26, which tradition attributes to King Solomon. Discuss the writer's attitude about work.

A Prayer from You

. . .

9

BUCKLE UP! LIFE'S ROLLER COASTER
GETS BUMPY SOMETIMES

My child, don't turn away or become bitter when the LORD corrects you. The LORD corrects everyone he loves, just as parents correct their favorite child. (Proverbs 3:11-12, CEV)

God's correction is always right and for our best good, that we may share his holiness. Being punished isn't enjoyable while it is happening—it hurts! But afterwards we can see the result, a quiet growth in grace and character. (Hebrews 12:10-11, CEV)

My Dear One,

Many years ago, I heard a very wise minister, Rev. Robert Culp of the First Church of God in Toledo, Ohio, preach a series of sermons about the Twenty-third Psalm. I hope you find his thoughts as comforting, educational, enlightening, and funny as I did!

Rev. Culp reminded his audience that sheep, much like humans, are dumb animals; they will follow anyone who stands before them and looks like he or she knows where to go—even if that individual doesn't have a clue. Sheep are helpless, without sharp claws, beaks, or any kind of natural defenses. If and when they fall, they cannot get up without help. If not carefully watched, they will wander off and get themselves into all kinds of trouble. They have poor vision and lack judgment. They can easily eat too much and get sick. When they drink, the water must come from a source that is calm and peaceful. They must look to their shepherd for everything.

The Twenty-third Psalm begins with the words "The LORD is my shepherd." This means that not only is God our creator and provider, but our protector and nurturer as well. We are God's sheep. Think about what it means to be a sheep!

Rev. Culp continued to explain that when lambs are first born and getting up on their legs, in their innocence and friskiness, they run around, stray, and run off, which sometimes puts them in distress, trouble, or even life-threatening circumstances. Because they are so young, they don't yet know the shepherd's voice or how to obey the shepherd's commands. For this reason, the shepherd will break a lamb's legs, bind them together, and then carry the lamb on his (or her) shoulders. While the lamb's legs are healing, it is totally dependent upon the shepherd for everything—movement, food, water, care, etc. It becomes the first to hear the voice of the shepherd. It can feel the shepherd's shoulders tighten and tense up with worry about the other sheep. It can feel the shepherd's shoulders move up and down in laughter and joy when the other sheep do something funny. It is the first to feel the gentleness of the shepherd's touch when he or she lifts it up or puts it down. The lamb gets to know, respond to, and love the shepherd, even though that intimacy develops in a period of discomfort and pain.

When the lamb's legs are healed and it is up on its legs again, the most important person to that young lamb is, again, the shepherd. That's why the sheep automatically respond to the shepherd's voice and commands. They know that voice, trust and believe in it.

As you grow up and God disciplines you, think of yourself as one of God's lambs who is out there, sometimes a little too frisky, running around. As the Good Shepherd, Jesus will break your legs—by allowing hard and troubling times to come to you. He will bind you up and then carry you on his shoulders so he can teach you about staying close to him, obeying his commands, and recognizing his care, love, and protection. Jesus will also teach you the sound of his voice so that you can respond in obedience when you hear it.

Experiencing difficult times is not fun or easy, but it is necessary for your growth and spiritual maturity. The ultimate security is the knowledge that when you are experiencing the broken-leg times, a loving God, the Good Shepherd, is always close at hand, carrying you.

A Prayer for You

Precious Jesus, the Great Shepherd of us all,

How grateful we are that, as your children, you have given us the assurance that you will not leave us or forsake us.

I pray for this child as she grows, moves, matures, and has her legs broken from time to time. Bind her legs and lift her to your shoulders. Carry her in your loving arms. Breathe on her so she will instinctively know that she is feeling you and that she is your little lamb and you are her very Good Shepherd. Guide her steps as her legs heal and help her to learn the sound of your voice. Give her understanding so she might learn to accept that the hard times come to make her strong, and that since you are with her, guiding and always protecting her, she has nothing to fear. Amen.

For Your Consideration

1. List some characteristics of sheep. Which of those characteristics do you have in common with them?
2. Read John 10:1-18. What are the characteristics of the Good Shepherd?
3. Write down some situations where God has been your Good Shepherd.

A Prayer from You

. . .

10

P.U.S.H.

PRAY UNTIL SOMETHING HAPPENS

"Everything you ask for in prayer will be yours, if you only have faith. Whenever you stand up to pray, you must forgive what others have done to you. Then your Father in heaven will forgive your sins." (Mark 11:24-26, CEV)

And in the same way—by our faith—the Holy Spirit helps us with our daily problems and in our praying. For we don't even know what we should pray for, or how to pray as we should; but the Holy Spirit prays for us with such feeling that it cannot be expressed in words. (Romans 8:26, TLB)

My Dear One,

Prayer is the act of talking to and with God. It is a pouring out of your soul or crying out to God for help as well as for thanksgiving. For Christians, prayer is not something we *try* to do; it is what we *do*—on a daily basis. Christ prayed and provided a model prayer (sometimes called "The

Lord's Prayer") for us as Christians to follow (Matthew 6:9-13; Luke 12:2-4). You may have learned it when you were small; however, as you grow it takes on a new, deeper, and richer meaning. Its words deserve much more attention. Every now and then read it out loud—slowly—and listen to the words.

The traditional version, as recorded in Matthew 6:9-13 (KJV), begins: "Our Father, which art in heaven, Hallowed be thy name. Thy kingdom come. Thy will be done..." Wait, back up. Don't pass that!

Thy will be done. That's an important line. When we as Christians pray this prayer, we are telling God that in spite of our requests and pleas for "stuff," we realize and accept the fact that only God knows what is right for us. We tell God that we know he has our best interests at heart—in our lives, our relationships, our work, our education, our futures. God knows what we need, when we need it, what we can handle, and what must be present in our lives in order for us to become the people that he needs us to be. We also acknowledge that God is the only one who can provide those things. We only know what (we think) we want. And let's face it: Most of our wants are things that will be out of style tomorrow!

"Thy will be done in earth, as it is in heaven..." God reigns *everywhere*—period!

"Give us this day our daily bread. And forgive us our debts [our sins, our wrongs] as we forgive our debtors [those who have wronged us]." A word of caution here: Don't be too quick to say these words and proceed to the end of the prayer! Forgiveness is powerful. It is also difficult to do sometimes. But, God forces us to examine it and then challenges us to make very clear decisions about it. Jesus tells us if we can't forgive others (as well as ourselves), then God cannot forgive us (Matthew 11:25-26). We cannot want for ourselves that which we deny to others (Matthew 7:12). It doesn't work like that.

Forgiveness heals—you, as well as the person who needs to be forgiven. Forgiving that person helps *you* to sleep better at night, to digest your food, to keep your blood pressure normal. It keeps you smiling and laughing. It brings joy and peace to your heart and spirit. It helps you to move forward by helping you to see and work on your own failings and shortcomings. Ask God to teach you not only to love, but to forgive as well. Let it be something that you choose to do on a daily basis.

"And lead us not into temptation but deliver us from evil: For thine is the kingdom, and the power, and the glory, forever." *Amen.*

This model prayer teaches us that there is a way in which we must approach the throne of God, by recognizing (1) God's majesty and power, (2) God's control over everything, (3) God's provision for our daily needs, (4) God's power of forgiveness and deliverance, and (5) that God is all.

When you think about it, this prayer covers all of the basics. It's like a circle that begins and ends at exactly the same point. And like a circle, God's love for us (for you) has no beginning and no end; it is eternal.

You might also have noticed that there isn't a single place in this model prayer where we get to put all of our "God-I-want," "Lord-can-I-have," "But-Lord-if-I-could-only-get" requests. Isn't God smart!

As you grow in your knowledge of God, your prayer life must also develop and grow so that your spiritual temple grows stronger. You will begin to understand that you must pray for a heart that is sincere and not to pray out of selfish desire (James 4:3).

You will learn not to limit yourself to the model prayer of Jesus but to discover that there is much to thank God for and discuss with him. Pray for your family and your friends, name by name; for your church family, your neighbors, your neighborhoods, and your teachers. Pray for our government and our world. Pray for peace and the end of suffering and oppression of all kinds. Pray for God's healing power for those who are sick, ailing, and bereaved. Pray for those who are incarcerated as well as for those in the prisons of fear, anger, and depression. Pray for those who do not know God and are lost in their sins. Pray for yourself. Pray for guidance, wisdom, and direction in your life and in your living. Pray for love and obedience, for patience, courage, and strength. Pray for cleanliness of mind, heart, spirit, purpose, and speech. Pray for forgiveness of your sins, of the sins of others toward you, and for daily cleansing of the interior of your temple so that God will continually live there and be happy and pleased with the space!

A Prayer for You

Father God,

Turn your ears towards the prayer of your child as she learns to speak to you. Help her to understand that it is not the easy flow of words, the grandness of her vocabulary, or the catchy phrases that she may have heard others say that will impress you. For you are not interested in being impressed with words but with the sincerity of her heart as she opens it up and presents it to you. Bring all of the things that she needs to pray for to her mind and spirit. Help her to never grow weary of spending time with you in this way. Show her that *you* must be a priority.

Keep her friends, her teachers, her family, all who are so important in her life. Bless her enemies and make them no longer stumbling blocks but stepping stones. Teach her the importance of asking for forgiveness for herself and for others. Teach her to keep her eyes stayed on you and her heart ready to receive your will for her life.

Then, Lord, teach her patience so that she might listen to you. In Jesus' name, I pray. Amen.

For Your Consideration

1. Due to Supreme Court rulings on prayer, many schools now observe a "moment of silence." If your school has such a policy, what do you do with your "moment"?
2. Read James 4:3. How does this passage apply to you?

A Prayer from You

. . .

• 11 •

WORK

BEES DO IT, ANTS DO IT...

Whatever you do, work at it with all your heart, as working for the Lord, not for men, since you know that you will receive an inheritance from the Lord as a reward. It is the Lord Christ you are serving. (Colossians 3:23-24, NIV)

Six days you shall labor and do all your work, but the seventh day is a Sabbath to the LORD your God. On it you shall not do any work...therefore the LORD blessed the Sabbath day and made it holy. (Exodus 20:9-11, NIV)

My Dear One,

At some point in time, in the not-too-distant future, you will probably become interested in having your own money, buying your own stuff, and making your own financial decisions. That will be the time when (if you haven't done so already) you will want to get a job and will begin to experience the world of work. This is normal and expected. After all, you probably have grown up with that word *work* and the images of people leaving and returning from work. And, you wish to share in the experience.

Well, my darlin', God has a lot to say about work and working. In fact, the work that God has assigned us to do through and for him, God regards as his fields (see Matthew 9:38 and 1 Corinthians 3:9). And, it is within these fields—God's world—that we work to feed, clothe, care for, educate, defend, nurture, and support God's children.

Before you begin to look for your first "real" job (one that might involve a uniform or a time clock!), be careful and prayerful about the world of work. You are standing on the edge of an experience that will occupy a great deal of your adult life. Perhaps this first work venture will be a glimpse into the future career that God has planned for you. Perhaps it will introduce you to people who will teach you the value of developing a strong work ethic and good work habits. Or, perhaps this first experience will demonstrate those things that you should *not* do as an employee (for example, have a poor attitude or learn to be a workaholic with no real purpose in life outside the job). Remember, these work experiences have already been well thought out and designed by God in order to mold and shape you into becoming the worker God needs in his fields, his world. He has plans for you and needs you to be prepared.

Your entry into this world of work will include being compensated or *paid* every week or two. Don't get carried away by thinking that your paycheck is all the money there is. It isn't; it's just all the money that you have earned that has your name written on it! And, don't let Satan tempt you into believing "I work. It's *my* money, and *no one* tells *me* what to do with it!" Darlin', don't go there. It's called ego, and it's not good. The real deal about that? It's God's money, just as the work, the labor, the job—everything you have—belongs to God. The same way that God blesses you with employment opportunities and paychecks, God also has the power to remove those blessings if you don't appreciate how to handle them. Learn to be humble and grateful for the job and the salary you earn for your labor. Additionally, don't make the mistake of believing that you must be paid for anything and everything you do. Volunteering your time is worthwhile—especially if you can't get a job right away. A school or community center, a nursing home or hospital, a church or shelter are also parts of God's field, and he has much to teach you as you learn to give of yourself.

Ask God to teach you how to handle your earnings—and your time—wisely. Learn now the importance of tithing, giving back to God 10 percent (at the minimum)—that's ten cents of every dollar of your income each and every time you are paid. Don't take this lightly or dismiss it easily. God will give you the health and strength to get to and from the job, and he will give you the good sense and the grace to realize that you are indebted to him, not just for the opportunity of employment but for your intellect, your education, and your personality—all the qualities you need in order to keep the job.

Honor God in your work and do not neglect to go to his house, the church, to praise him for blessing you in this way. Rise early each morning and thank God for providing you with employment, a place of work, colleagues, and people who support the need for you to have a job in the first place—your customers! Go to work on time, with a positive attitude and a cheerful disposition. Since God blesses you with health and strength, let your movements reflect that.

At paycheck time, show your gratitude and praise (God does love a cheerful giver!), first by tithing and then by saving a portion (another 10 percent, perhaps). Learn to budget for your needs (personal hygiene stuff, transportation, school supplies, etc.). Look for opportunities to share with your family the benefits of your job. Buy a pizza for dinner every now and then; put some gas in the family car, or contribute something toward a bill. (You live there too remember?)

Do something thoughtful for someone else, such as sending a card to a church member, relative, or elderly neighbor. Perform a random act of kindness at least once every payday. It could be something as simple as paying bus fare for a stranger...or purchasing each member of your Sunday school class (of course you go to Sunday school!) a Christian bookmark...or buying a thank-you card for the pastor of your church—just because. Then treat yourself to something special each paycheck: a book, body lotion, bubble bath, manicure or pedicure, or a bunch of fresh flowers.

These gestures—for others and for yourself—don't have to be expensive, but they will teach you all of the ways that God blesses you, and then you share those blessings with others. Your gifts will make the people in your life feel good—and make you feel even better! You will also learn valuable habits of self-love and care.

Of course, work entails more than just a paycheck. You will be challenged to live faithfully on the job, as well as outside of it. So don't get caught up in office and workplace garbage. Behaviors such as gossiping, backbiting, talking back to supervisors (a.k.a., insubordination!), fostering negative attitudes, etc., pollute the air, stifle the spirit, choke off everyone's productivity, and make Satan happy. To God, however, such negativity is seen as "sowing discord among the brethren" (Proverbs 6:16-19, KJV), and that is one of the behaviors God hates. So, don't participate in it.

Finally, remember that when you work, it will not be to please other people (although you will have a boss to answer to). You will be working for a higher Boss with very high standards and expectations and all of the means to help you reach both. (That goes for schoolwork, too!) Honor that Heavenly Boss by keeping the Sabbath as God's day. If and when you are given the choice of working or being off on Sundays, choose "off" and get yourself to church—not out of duty but out of thanksgiving. Think about it: You've been blessed with a lot!

A Prayer for You

Dear God,

This is your child, your daughter. Prepare her for the day when she will enter the world of work. Open her mind and spirit to learning how to be a good worker. Open her ears for listening, her mind for understanding, her spirit for accepting and learning from her mistakes. Give her humility to realize that work—large and small tasks—is honorable and blessed by you. Teach her to give cheerfully and unselfishly.

Lead her to managers and employers, coworkers and colleagues who know you, honor you, and revere you, so that you may be seen in the ways they handle themselves.

Give them patience and a willing spirit to teach her and assist in her development as a worker—ready, willing, and able to do the work you have in her future. Bless the homes and families of her coworkers, as well as the work of their hands as they, too, labor in your vineyard. In Jesus' name we pray. Amen.

For Your Consideration

1. Read 2 Thessalonians 3:10. What does this mean to workers? To you?
2. Read Luke 10:7. How does this apply to supervisors? To you?

A Prayer from You

■ ■ ■

PART THREE

THE REAL DEAL

ON CHALLENGES TO CONSTRUCTION

12

INGRATITUDE

DON'T GET CAUGHT IN THIS TRAP!

There is a way that seems right to a man, but in the end it leads to death. (Proverbs 14:12, NIV)

And as for you brothers (sisters), never tire of doing what is right. (2 Thessalonians 3:13, NIV)

My Dear One,

We live in a society that moves very quickly—so quickly that if we are not careful, we will find ourselves trying to move and keep up with it. We are told that since everything is fast and available now, there is no need to wait for anything. For example, the culture teaches young people that one is considered an adult when one can drive, smoke, drink, have sex, be sexual, and have credit cards. Isn't it interesting how more and more teens are doing more and more of these kinds of things before they actually reach the age of adulthood? And how even younger and younger children are being introduced to these same kinds of things? Think about it.

Look closely at the music videos that play constantly. Pay attention to the pop stars (particularly the "divas") who star in them. Have you noticed that as many of these young women move closer to the age of twenty-one (the age of adulthood), they wear fewer and fewer clothes? They become thinner and far more sexual in their movements as they sing and dance. Suddenly the young girls who *were* about your age and could relate to you are now women.

On the other hand, the vast majority of the guys and rappers who appear in these same kinds of videos keep all of their clothes on. As they begin to get older, they either become more romantic and sensitive or take on a macho, "bad boy," roughneck image. They are suddenly men.

As these young stars attempt to break into this adult world, you begin to see them in other places—commercials, print ads, TV shows, and movies. For many, as they age they become vulnerable, and for survival's sake, in order to remain profitable, they have to become interesting (more adult?) to an older crowd. If you attend their concerts, you may not see very much of the stars themselves, but you will see wonderful light shows, flash, and spectacle.

The newspapers keep you informed about their weekly loves and intimate entanglements. You see their rich and lavish lifestyles, their homes and cars. You read about their multimillion dollar contracts. You buy their posters and calendars. You log on to their websites. You listen to their interviews, in which they declare that they are nothing like the images that they portray. How many of them talk about how quiet, shy, and unassuming they really are? How many of them are still around after about two years and three hit singles?

In fact, how many songs, stars, groups, etc., can you name that have been around for longer than two years and are still as popular now as they were when they first appeared? Kind of makes you go "hmm," doesn't it?

How many young people such as yourself spend their days, nights, and too much of their time dreaming, wishing, and hoping that they were just like these stars?

And, let's not forget the world of the athletes. How many young black males have only one thing on their minds— playing professional ball! How many teens are ignoring schoolwork, holding back in class, and pushing aside education altogether in the hope and dream that they will become the next football or basketball wonder athlete, rapper, or pop diva? How many are looking for the celebrity status of others and totally ignoring their own skills, talents, and abilities?

Oh, my darlin', is Satan having a ball with this one!

Proverbs 14:12 says, "There is a way that seems right to man but in the end, leads to death" (NIV). This is not just talking about physical death but other kinds of death: the death of one's spirit, the death of one's hopes and dreams, the death of one's self-esteem, and the death of innocence. Darlin', pay attention because there are a couple of things going on here.

First, there is the issue of covetousness rearing its ugly head—again. (We covered this back in Chapter 3.) Covetousness has to do with that constant longing, pining, and whining to have what others have—others such as the pop stars, rappers, and athletes.

In most cases, if teens were honest, they don't particularly want to do the "work" that these folks have had to do. Isn't it really about the stuff that they have? Let's face it:

How many years of practice did it take for someone like Michael Jordan to become the athlete he has been? How many missed shots at the hoop? How many tears shed at lost games? And the movie stars…? How many church skits or high-school and college plays did they have to perform in, how many auditions were they rejected in, how many commercials did they go out for, and how many tables did they have to wait before they became an "overnight" success? No, my darlin', the stuff that they own is the easy part. Don't let Satan fool you. Fame and fortune ain't that easy; they're tough to come by. And *staying* on top is even harder than getting there in the first place! (Remember that list of stars who aren't stars anymore?)

Second, there's the issue of regrets. When interviewed, how many of these celebrities talk about the ordinary things in life that *you* have but that *they* can no longer enjoy? Things such as going to school with peers, hanging out at the mall with friends, playing sports with a team? Ain't it fascinating how, so often, we spend our lives desiring the things of others, and they spend their time desiring our lives! Now do you understand why God says to be grateful for what blessings you already possess?

Open your eyes, my darlin'. It's fun to run behind the celebrities…to know their songs or game statistics, to go to their movies and concerts. But remember this: Like you, they are God's children. God does not love them any more or any less than God loves you. Their fame and fortune have nothing to do with his regard for them.

Forget the "hoochie mamas" and rappers from the videos, the pop stars, and the athletes! God does not want you skipping over your adolescence and all of the experiences those years will bring in order for you suddenly to become an adult. Remember: Adult behavior brings on adult responsibilities. Don't miss out on your special blessings by trying to get someone else's. You will lose each and every time.

Your time will come. Learn to be grateful and satisfied with all that God has given to you, great and small. Those who miss, ignore, and belittle God's blessings tend to lose them. Don't lose yours, because the Lord has wonderful, exciting, fantastic blessings just for you (Jeremiah 29:11). Be patient and stay tuned!

A Prayer for You

God of All,

What a blessing to have you in control of our lives. How wonderful to know that you have set aside many wonderful, new, and exciting experiences, places, and people—just for us. Words of thanks are so inadequate, but we do say thank you, Lord.

Keep this child grounded, calm, and focused. Hold her in check when she would get carried away with the celebrities of the world and think too much about them and not enough about you. Teach her to honor and revere you.

Teach her to love herself, her gifts, her talents, her abilities, and her temple. Push her to learn more about the wonder that she is...the woman she is becoming. Help her to apply herself in school, to not grow lazy, stubborn, or obstinate but to keep her eyes and heart open to the experiences that you shower down on her daily.

You have promised her that you have plans for her; plans that will show the world what an awesome person she is. Remind her, Lord, that she is not cut from a cookie cutter to be a replica of anyone else, but that she is an original, one of a kind. I pray that she will grow to value the knowledge and understanding of that. In Jesus' name, I pray. Amen.

For Your Consideration

1. Name three celebrities who were popular three years ago. Where are they now? Name three who were popular last year. Where are they now?
2. Read Psalm 34:8-14. How does this apply to you and your future?

A Prayer from You

■ ■ ■

13

REVENGE

DON'T EVEN THINK ABOUT IT!

Get rid of all bitterness, rage and anger, brawling and slander, along with every form of malice. Be kind and compassionate to one another, forgiving each other, just as in Christ God forgave you. (Ephesians 4:31-33, NIV)

My Dear One,

How often have you come home from school feeling hurt and angry over something that happened? Perhaps someone teased you about your clothes, your hair, or your body? Or someone tried to get really "loud" on you in class? Or someone you thought of as a friend suddenly decided to trash your reputation? Or maybe a negative rumor about you became gossip that followed you around all day?

So, you have escaped to the comfort of a space that is yours alone, and you feel all the emotions at once: anger, frustration, hurt, pain, fear, and betrayal. How do you handle it? What do you do with all that *stuff*?

Well, my darlin', it's important to acknowledge the fact that what has happened is indeed hurtful. It hurts when people talk about you and say all kinds of ugly, unkind, and untruthful things about you. Let's face it. When we enter the world, about the only things that come with us (other than our bodies) are our given names and our reputations. Both are very precious to us. What can take a lifetime to build up can be destroyed within a matter of minutes through rumors, innuendoes, and lies. Check out the latest editions of the daily newspapers to prove my point.

While you are in that space that is yours, allow yourself to feel the pain and have yourself a real good cry. Not just that sissy sniffling stuff where you try your best to be strong and really mature and swallow it (that comes later) but the kind of cry where your face is all messed up, your nose runs, and you need a towel because tissues just won't do! Yeah, like that. Cry it all out until you get tired of crying. Then, think of something that was said about you that was so incredibly stupid even you have to laugh at it. Then do just that: laugh so long and so hard that you are crying again—from laughter. Can you imagine anyone actually believing that garbage?

Why do people spend their time and energy spreading gossip and lies? Why do some folks seem to get such joy out of spreading that "she-said-you-said-I-said" trash? Why do some folks allow themselves to be used in such a wasteful kind of way? And, why do other folks go along with it? Is Satan busy or what? There are a few things for you to keep in mind when confronted with this kind of stupidity.

First, the real deal is that you cannot go through life explaining, defending, apologizing, and trying to justify yourself to people who do this kind of stuff. God's Word is right to the point on this. It says in Proverbs "whoever spreads slander [lies] is a fool" (10:18, NIV) and "only fools love to quarrel" (20:3, CEV).

Second, God says that he detests "lying, murdering, plotting evil, eagerness to do wrong, a false witness, and sowing discord among brothers" (Proverbs 6:16-19, TLB). That's not just discord among people who are related by blood, but people who are related by purpose and spirit; like you and your friends. God says he hates this kind of behavior because it creates disruption, confusion, pain, and unnecessary hassles. Believe him.

Third, despite the fact that folks will talk about you and try to get up in your face, stay mindful of the fact that you are God's child. Therefore, you must live as God commands you to live and act as he commands you to act. When and if these negative and hurtful things happen, take a deep breath. Hold your tongue, keep your head up high, whisper a prayer to Jesus for strength—this is when you really need it—and in the words of the famous comedian, Jay Anthony Brown, let them watch you as "you walk awaaaay!" Don't indulge in "hatred and fighting, jealousy and anger, constant efforts to get the best for yourself, complaints and criticisms" (Galatians 5:20, TLB). Instead of fighting fire with fire or returning evil for evil, Christians are taught by God to do two things.

1. Demonstrate those things that are called fruits of the spirit: love, joy, peace, patience, kindness, goodness, faithfulness, gentleness, and self-control (Galatians 5:22)—all things the world tells us *not* to demonstrate. The Bible tells us that when we are kind to our enemies, it is like "piling burning coals on their heads. And the Lord will reward you" (Proverbs 25:22, CEV). So, watch them squirm under the heat! Deep, huh? And no, it's not as wimpy as it might sound. It is going to require courage, guts, and determination on your part.

2. Let God handle the situation. Let the Lord represent. Trust him to have your back. God promises "It is mine to avenge; I will repay. In due time their foot will slip; their day of disaster is near and their doom rushes upon them" (Deuteronomy 32:35, NIV). My darlin', I can promise you this: What God has in mind for them you could not think of in a million nights of staying up late, plotting and scheming. You can trust God (and me!) on that! You just do what you are called to do and be patient. You may not see it, but justice is coming. No one gets away with anything.

I know this is not easy to do, but don't worry or spend a lot of time stressing out about those things said about you that are negative, vicious, and downright false. Again, it will take courage, prayer, patience, and faith in God to deal with it. Don't stay up nights thinking, planning, and praying for a response to it. There is no response. Instead, learn how to forgive the ones who have treated you badly. That's right: forgive them and pray for them. They'll need it.

Besides, you will find that the most important people in your life—your true friends—and even those who don't know you personally but who have checked you out from a distance—don't believe that stuff anyway. Learn to ignore the negative, and do not give it (or Satan) a place of importance in your life. It takes up too much time and space from the positive.

I heard a very wise minister, Pastor Joe B. Fleming, from the Third Baptist Church in Portsmouth, Virginia, say that God also has a reputation. When Satan and his demons (all that negative stuff) rise up to hurt God's children (like you), God's reputation of caring, loving, protecting, forgiving, providing, and even avenging is being tested. The same way you wish to do everything in your power to make sure *your* reputation stays whole and clean, God does the same with his reputation. When you trust God and try to live as he wants you to live, God's rep is on the line. The Lord cannot fail. He must prevail. God has a reputation to protect!

Oh, yeah, and that good cry that you just had? It will help you get some of the best sleep of your life! What Satan meant for your pain and suffering, God turns into a beauty treatment! Ain't God grand?

A Prayer for You

Father in Heaven,

How easy it is to return evil for evil when we are wronged. How simple and right it sometimes seems to us to take matters into our own hands and solve our disputes in our own way. How wrong we are in this kind of thinking when we as your children have been taught through your Word about the actions, attitudes, and behaviors we must have. You tell us to bring the problems, the hurts, the pain *to* you—and leave it *with* you…that you and only you know how to take care of the situation. It is not easy, Lord.

So, Father, I pray now for your daughter and those times when she will feel embarrassment, pain, and betrayal because of gossip, rumors, and untruths…for those times when her reputation—and yours—will be on the line. I pray that she will heed your Spirit's exhortation to stop and not engage in simple and easy retaliation—but to listen and be comforted, knowing that you are aware of her situation and that you are in control. Give her clarity of mind, heart, and focus on those things that are good and are of you.

Lead and guide her as she chooses her friends and associates. Give her wisdom and discernment as she encounters situations and people that are new, different, and sometimes difficult. Strengthen her for those times. Teach her to pray for her enemies as well as for her friends. Help her to learn to forgive others so that she might understand the value and importance of forgiveness. Make her sensitive so that she can be supportive of those who encounter the same kinds of hurts that she encounters. May she be strength for them.

Remind her that you never leave, neither do you forsake. Hold her close, dry her tears, lift her head high, and swiftly send joy to her. In Jesus' name, I ask all these things. Amen.

For Your Consideration

1. Read James 3. How does this apply to your enemies? How does it apply to you?
2. Read Proverbs 10:18-19. Think about those times when you have been guilty of participating in these kinds of actions. Make a list of people to whom you need to apologize and then apologize to them.

A Prayer from You

■ ■ ■

14

NEGATIVITY

PIGEONS AREN'T THE ONLY ONES THAT WILL DROP STUFF ON YOUR TEMPLE!

Last of all I want to remind you that your strength must come from the Lord's mighty power within you.... For we are not fighting against people made of flesh and blood, but against persons without bodies—the evil rulers of the unseen world, those mighty satanic beings and great evil princes of darkness who rule this world; and against huge numbers of wicked spirits in the spirit world. (Ephesians 6:10,12, TLB)

My Dear One,

The gifted short-story writer J. California Cooper (check out her books from the library) made a statement in a presentation at a writer's conference once. She said that there were all kinds of people in the world, and that some of those people carry "little bags of 'doo-doo'" in their brains, watching and looking for someone to dump the bags of 'doo-doo' on. They just don't pick anybody," she continued. "No, they look for happy people to dump the bags of 'doo-doo.' If you are happy, don't let them dump the 'doo-doo' on you!"

You can imagine how we all screamed with laughter at that mental picture. But when you really begin to think about it, it makes a lot of sense. There are all kinds of people out there, and many of them are looking for just the right person to dump their *stuff* on. Quite often it happens slowly, subtly. Many times in our innocence, we welcome it.

These kinds of people (males as well as female!) are like the parasites that you study in your science classes. These human parasites rob you of your love of life and joy. They siphon off your capacity to give and share. They suck out your laughter and snuff out the light in your eyes. You probably don't recognize that, because *they* are never happy, satisfied, contented with anything, slowly over time then neither are you. They find fault with everything and everybody. They are critical and constantly looking for the worst in others. They always know the most awful things about other people. No one is pretty, smart, talented, nice, good, etc. According to them, no one is "all that" or has anything "going on" (which, by the way, includes them). These people spread gossip, rumors, and lies as if they were facts. (Remember the last chapter?)

You might accept these "doo-doo" dumpers/parasites into your life, and then in time you will find that you are feeling tired and drained. You lack energy and interest in the things that you used to love. It is a chore and a burden to get up in the mornings. You don't smile anymore. You feel sad and look even sadder. Your feelings of anger, frustration, and bitterness have led to feelings of depression. You don't realize that these people whom you have so willingly welcomed into your life (sometimes because of your own desire to "fit in") are negative and small, and that you are becoming the same way. You don't realize that they have dumped their "doo-doo bags" in your life, and you have embraced them—the doo-doo bags and the dumper! Think about it.

That, my darlin', is Satan and the way he works.

Satan is the negative spirit that moves and operates around us. It is a spirit designed to cause confusion and anger, dissension and chaos, hurt and fear. It robs you of your focus. It cheats you of your attention to that which God has assigned you to do. It throws you curve balls. It mocks, undermines, and isolates you. It creates a barrier between you and those you love and care about, those that you could get to know—and God.

Sometimes, if you are not careful or diligent, the negative spirit can get within you and your temple. Understand that this negativity is not of God, and learn to recognize it when it presents itself. Listen to that voice inside you warning you of danger. That's the Holy Spirit living in your temple, reminding you that God is a jealous God and does not, *will not* occupy the same space as negativity.

Also understand that you all by yourself are powerless to deal with such a negative force. The good news is that you don't have to—you've got God, THE FORCE (yeah, like *Star Wars*). Don't let Satan (or his parasites) fool you. You need God every day and every hour to protect you from these kinds of negative forces. God stands ready to stop the negativity in its tracks when you call on him to do so. God will keep those forces from polluting your temple.

Rev. Dr. John Kinney, an eminent black theologian, says that when people of faith are truly in God's spirit, they are like "spiritual Tai Chi Masters"—never fighting these spirits because God and only God can do that, but always avoiding the blows. Think about that mental picture.

Happiness, joy, and peace are gifts of God that he wants you to experience in all areas of your life (Ecclesiastes 2:26; Galatians 5:22)—at school, at play, at church, and with your family. Don't surrender these gifts to the negative forces out there without a fight. That negativity is knocking at the doors of your temple, but do not let it in! You have a security system, remember?

Don't listen to the parasites who push you to join them in sitting around and talking about people—all day, every day. Don't join them when they want nothing for their own lives and even less for yours. Don't get sucked into developing a miserable attitude and then taking it out on others. Do your best work at school because God has given you the ability to do it and expects no less from you. God's got plans for you, girl!

Extend yourself and make friends with those who aren't necessarily in the popular crowd—even when it is difficult to do so. God will give you the courage and strength to do it. Stand up for what is good and right. Look around you and see how you can help others, and then do those things. Love your family for who and what they are—imperfect but yours. (You're in the family, too, you know!) Choose to embrace the good things in your life, thanking God daily for them and holding on—tightly—to them.

And since you know who those "doo-doo" baggers in your life are (come on, you know!), stay away from them!

A Prayer for You

Father God,

I love the way you guide and protect your children from those who would bring chaos and confusion into our lives.

What a joy to know that you are our strong defense, our shield, our "Force." I ask, Lord, that you open this child's eyes and give her a discerning spirit concerning the people who are a part of her daily life. Help her to interact with others in ways that glorify you and make you proud. Teach her to value and recognize not only the positives but the negatives as well, for it is within the negatives that she will see you and your mighty power at work to free her of that influence.

Touch those associated with her who are bound in negativity, and move her to pray for them. Work on her so that she will grow to understand the importance of keeping her temple free of negativity. In Jesus' name, I pray. Amen.

For Your Consideration

1. Read 2 Corinthians 11:14. What does this description mean to you?
2. Make a list of people you know whose behavior fits this description. Are you on the list?

A Prayer from You

. . .

15

INSECURITY, PART I

"TOO BLESSED TO BE STRESSED"

"Do not be like them [the pagans] for your Father knows what you need before you ask him." *(Matthew 6:8, NIV)*

My Dear One,

I want to revisit a topic I discussed earlier, but this time I shall cover it from a different perspective.

As a young woman (that's you) grows toward puberty (i.e., the time in life when you notice growth of underarm and pubic hair, breast development, onset of menstrual cycle, etc.), a lot of emotional growth begins to take place as well. Hundreds of questions begin to surface and become of maximum importance to you and your peers. Questions such as, What is love? How can you know it? How does it feel? Does it have to hurt for it to be real? Is it just like they say it is?

Excellent questions; not-so-easy answers—although reviewing Chapter 6 might help you make a start on them!

Often, young women look to the media for answers to these and other questions. However, when looking at TV, movies, music videos, and listening to popular music, one finds that the media sends all kinds of conflicting messages.

Singers and "rappers" spend vast amounts of time singing, crying, whining, weeping, bragging, begging, and boasting about the joys and difficulties of love. Despite the enormous popularity of soap operas, one would have to really look hard and long there to find examples of true love and happiness. These daytime-drama relationships are burdened with infidelity, dishonesty, disloyalty, adultery, lying, cheating, scheming—and those challenges are often folded into just one of several story lines! Music videos also demonstrate that perhaps it is not love that females really want, so much as it is getting a *man* (no boys allowed).

These media sources show that love means no more being alone or lonely because you have a male to hug, kiss, caress, and share things. Further, this so-called love is depicted as fragile, temporary, and subject to the (usually limited!) attention span of the lover. In other words, if the guy gets a little bored with you or sees someone else that he thinks has a few more "toys" to play with than you, you are doomed. Thus is the world's definition of *love*. How encouraging (not!).

As a result, women (both young and old) are miseducated by the media as to how we should go about pursuing males, who can be hard to get. According to the media/world, men are prizes to be hunted down and snared, by fair means or foul. And as women, we are to use whatever bait and enticements that will lure a man close enough for us to snatch him up and reel him in.

The fashion police and cosmetics industries join with the media to convince us that the way to bait our hook is to change ourselves—all over. Our necklines are to be cut down to our waistlines so our enlarged, padded, firmed, gelled, and siliconed breasts can hang out. Make-up should be used, applied, reapplied, and touched up yet again. Mascara is supposed to make our eyelashes long enough to sweep down and touch our lips, which are supposed to be full and pouty. We are to starve ourselves to pencil thinness, yet have shapely hips, butts, and legs to match our breasts (which are hanging out). Our skirts and shorts are to be shorter and shorter, tighter and tighter. Our blouses and tops get skimpier and more transparent. Our underwear gets smaller and covers less and less until the ideal becomes no underwear at all. The heels of our shoes get higher and higher, never thinking about the pressure it places on our backs. Our hair gets longer and longer or bought, dyed, braided, weaved, permed, and "tracked" with all the colors of the rainbow. Our nails are painted with even wilder colors and longer claw-like tips.

Even women's personalities are supposed to change. We are to be smart-dumb, aggressive-passive, understanding-demanding, tolerant-possessive, flirtatious-naïve, teasing-innocent, fragile-strong, pouty-funny, "easy"-hard to get, "good girl"-"bad-girl"—all at the same time! Psychologists call this schizophrenia; the world calls it getting a man!

We are encouraged to stake our claim on a guy (even the young ones!) and do any and everything to let other females know *our* man is not to be approached, looked at, spoken to, smiled at, or acknowledged in any way, shape, or form. It's like taking on the persona of a prison warden! We monitor his calls and question his whereabouts and his companions wherever he goes. We find any and all excuses to call (no matter the hour) and check up. We go by his house, his school locker, his classroom, the basketball court, his favorite hangout, and on and on. We threaten, confront, scream at, cuss out, and fight any female (even his mother!) who we think is staring at, trying to attract, or paying any attention to our man. A woman's cardinal rule is supposed to be: Trust no one and trust him even less than that.

Be and do all of these things according to the "world" (and the "hoochie mamas" out there), and you are practically guaranteed to get the guy—and love.

Oh, my darlin', those voices out there screaming at you ain't even close!

The real deal is this: God did not create women to be hunters. It goes against our nature and God's plan for our lives. Therefore, when we resort to such tactics we are met with, quite often, disaster and regrets. Sometimes the regrets last a lifetime.

Pay attention, my darlin'.

When you take on the role of hunter, you demonstrate lack of faith in God. You tell the Lord by your actions that you cannot fully trust him, because you refuse to place the responsibility of your future love life in his hands. Instead, you insist on handling things your way— the way of the world.

Don't allow yourself to get lured into thinking that God has gone off somewhere and has no idea of what is happening down here; that God simply does not understand how tough it is or how early one must begin to find and keep a man—especially in these days of such depressing statistics. Don't get caught up in what the world and its media tell you to do in order to accomplish the "all-important" goal of catching a man.

When you try to take control or your love life, you remove yourself from the love, care, and protection of God. You are like a spiritually lost lamb that has strayed from the shepherd, into lion's territory. You place yourself in a weak and vulnerable position. You are defenseless and prone to be used and abused. Be careful of lions that hang around sheep and claim to love them. They do—as the main course!

My darlin', God promises us that he will "meet all of our needs according to his glorious riches in Christ Jesus" (Philippians 4:19, NIV). God made us, so God knows that we need friendship and companionship and that we have the desire for a relationship. It is part of our divine design.

God is also more than a little aware of the body count on this planet—the exact number of available males and females. We don't need statistics to frighten us about the lack or abundance (in Alaska!) of good men.

Understand that for right now, today, your job is to concentrate on growing up, getting educated, having fun with your peers, developing spiritually, and preparing yourself for the work—and life—that God has set aside for you. The Word tells us not to worry about tomorrow; it will take care of itself (Matthew 6:34). When it is time for you to have a boyfriend or be in a relationship with someone special, God will take care of it. The Lord will choose the person, and he will create the time and place for you to meet. And, if it is God's will for your life that you marry someday, remember that while you are doing what you are supposed to be doing now, God is making the same preparations for that future young man—getting him ready for you. Trust God. He does have your future all mapped out (Jeremiah 29:11).

When you choose to believe that God does have very specific plans for your future, you live your life with less drama, less stress. You feel secure in God's assurances that he is in control, and you are free to focus on other things. Work on the doubts, fears, and shortcomings in yourself, so that you can be ready and receptive of the person God will send to you. Learn how to live your life reflective of the kinds of character traits—peace, joy, and contentment—that you desire to be surrounded by. There is no need to feel pressured, insecure, restless, isolated, strange, suspicious, jealous, threatened, or envious of others. Don't deal in the negatives, my darlin'. That's Satan, remember?

And when that day comes...the day that God has already assigned (if it is in his will) for you to meet "Mr. Right"? You'll be amazed at what you won't have to do to your hair, nails, neckline, hemline—or your personality!

A Prayer for You

O God,

Speak to your daughter when the way of the world appears to pass her by and causes confusion and doubt in her mind. Calm her fears so that she is not anxious or nervous about the pace of your plans and timing for her life. Assure her that you are close-by and know exactly what you are doing. Hold her back when she would run ahead of you; encourage her spirit when she would drag behind you; and keep her in check as you stand beside her, guiding and protecting her. Give her a receptive heart and yielding spirit to your will for her life. Bless her each day with courage, strength, and boldness to say yes to you and no to the world.

Forgive her (and the rest of us), Lord, for our times of little faith and trust in you. Give her more of both. We love you and all the ways you show your love to us. Make us worthy to live the glorious life that you have planned for each of us. In Jesus' name, I ask it all. Amen.

For Your Consideration

1. Read Psalm 139. What does God reveal to us about himself? What does God reveal about us?
2. Read Job 14:5. How does this apply to people? How does this apply to you?
3. Read Job 38. What does God reveal about us?

A Prayer from You

■ ■ ■

16

INSECURITY, PART II

SEPARATING THE "PAPER DOLLS" FROM THE REAL WOMEN OF GOD!

Your beauty should not come from outward adornment, such as braided hair and the wearing of gold jewelry and fine clothes. Instead, it should be that of your inner self, the unfading beauty of a gentle and quiet spirit, which is of great worth in God's sight. (1 Peter 3:3, NIV)

My Dear One,

In Chapter 12, I discussed the images promoted by the media and various celebrities to suggest that the way to demonstrate womanhood is to dress provocatively, thereby supposedly ensuring a female's ability to get a man or love.

Now before you go nuts (again!), my darlin', and say that I keep doggin' you girls, hear me out because there is a vital lesson you must get.

Many of today's female pop stars display a false sense of sexuality. In other words, they are perpetratin'. Most of these young women are far too young to know anything about the level of sex and sexuality that their songs and movements suggest. I am not saying that they are not sexually active (many could be); I am saying that they are too young to fully understand what they are talking about. They are simply mouthing words and projecting an image.

Come on, girl! Think! Don't let Satan play you like that! Don't allow him to mislead you into thinking that all of that bumpin' and grindin' is teaching you how to be a woman. Talking about sex, acting like you are having sex, and understanding sex are three very different things. These young women don't know or understand any more about their temples (yes, they have one too!), their bodies, and how they work than you do! My darlin', if they had a clue, they wouldn't allow themselves to be used in this way (even for the money).

Think about it. How much do you know about the biology of your body? What makes the female body such a wonder? What part do your emotions play in how your body functions? What are a woman's sexual "buttons"? Do you know where your fallopian tubes are? Why do you have them and what do they do? What about your clitoris—what is it and where is it? Why do you have a period, and what happens to your body before it begins? What about a fibroid—what is it and what does it have to do with black women? What's chlamydia? Toxemia? Why are black women (young and not-so-young) all over the world dying from AIDS? Why is it that some days of the month you are on top of the world, and other times you are as evil as a snake? Why is chocolate so important to women? Biologically, physically, emotionally, psychologically, and spiritually, what makes a woman a *woman?*

Well, the real deal, my darlin', is that REAL WOMEN, empowered women—women of God—are at their sexiest and most "fly" when they know their temples...the interior as well as the exterior...the biology, emotions, and psychology of being a woman. And that takes knowledge, age, experience, and time. In other words, you *grow* into becoming a woman. One event (losing your virginity or having a baby) does not make you a woman. I don't care what the songs say!

REAL WOMEN are intelligent because they are smart and wise enough to know that brains and intellect are from God and are to be used under his direction. They are confident because they know that they are daughters of the King and that, as his child, they are blessed to be special and one of a kind. They dress modestly and in good taste because as the "King's kid" there is no reason to advertise or flaunt any part of their bodies. They are not hunting for anybody or anything—especially not for males who are out looking for "hoochie mamas." REAL WOMEN know and understand that they are far too loved, too precious, and too together for that.

Women of God know and understand that pop stars don't *feel* the sexiness that they are acting. They know that you are seeing "paper dolls" who are dressed up to look like sexual toys, the figments of men's (hormonal) imaginations. All of that panting, rubbing, and breathing...give me a break! It's advertising and it sells—a lot.

REAL WOMEN know that paper dolls are cheap, disposable, and replaceable!

And REAL WOMEN—especially REAL WOMEN of God—know that they are none of the above!

Girl, REAL WOMEN don't fall for Satan's okey doke!

You've got some homework to do! So, get busy learning about your temple—the interior as well as the exterior. (Hey, isn't this how we started?) Pay attention in health and science classes; this is *your* body they are talking about. Honor it, respect it, and learn how to take care of it. Ask questions. Go to the library and check out books on the human body (female and male). Learn about the changes the female body goes through on its way to becoming a woman. Talk to your doctor. Learn about the appropriate age and stage of female development for having children. Read God's Word and begin to understand the reasons why God intended sex to be practiced within marriage.

Begin now, my darlin', to learn what it means for your body to be the temple of the living God. Let it be the site where God can spread out his comfort, peace, and joy. Let it be the place where the welcome mat is always extended and where your heart is always open to God's presence. Let it be the place that God calls home. You do all of that, and you will become not just a woman but a REAL WOMAN of God—and that's the real deal!

A Prayer for You

Father God,

I praise you and honor you for all the ways that you grow us up to be the women that you want us to be. It is not an easy road, but you constantly assure us that you are with us.

I thank you for this child, your daughter. I ask your guidance and protection for her as she struggles to learn all of the many facets of her temple. May she always seek your direction and grace in all that she does. Forgive her sins, her shortcomings, and all of the ways that she might be misled and confused by the noise and clamor of the world. Help her to heed the examples around her and choose your ways. Help her to be a Joshua: strong and courageous, not looking to the left or right but always up to you. Teach her what it means to be a REAL WOMAN for you. Place women who model such behavior in her path so that she will know that to live for you is worth doing— that it is possible and attainable.

I love you, Lord, and I love the way that you love and care for us all—especially this child. Open her eyes to those things that you do. Keep her close and may she always want you, the guardian of her temple. In Jesus' name, I pray. Amen.

For Your Consideration

1. Read Esther 1:1–2:1. What does Queen Vashti teach us about womanhood?
2. Read Proverbs 31:10-31. Does this example of womanhood exist today? Why or why not?

A Prayer from You

. . .

17

SEX AND SEXUALITY

OK, DARLIN', THIS IS THE REAL DEAL!

That is why I say to run from sex sin. No other sin affects the body as this one does. When you sin this sin it is against your own body. (1 Corinthians 6:18, TLB)

"Do not give dogs what is sacred; do not throw your pearls to pigs. If you do, they may trample them under their feet, and then turn and tear you to pieces." (Matthew 7:6, NIV)

My Dear One,

Don't let the world (the media, etc.) fool you. *Sex is a big deal to God!* And God does not appreciate the way it has been distorted, twisted, and misrepresented by the world. It ticks him off.

My darlin', listen closely: The Word of God states that when God created Adam and Eve, they became one flesh (Genesis 2:23-24). They became one, not only in marital union, but one in sexual union as well. Yes, it's biology and physiology, but it is also psychology and spirituality. Sex is not just about what the body feels, but also what the mind thinks and the heart expresses, and the emotional response to it all.

God wants sex in marriage because it takes time, care, and attention to learn what pleases and provides pleasure for a spouse. It is the ultimate form of giving between two individuals who have stood before God seeking his blessing to become one. It is also the highest form of mutual pleasure that two people within that marriage can share. God says that since the two have become one, they have the rest of their lives ("till death us do part") to grow together, to learn each other, to touch and feel, to understand, to play, and to "get it right" with each other. God says that taking a relationship to a deeper level of love, understanding, and intimacy is the greatest—and sometimes most challenging—part of marriage. That kind of giving, sharing, concern, and loving exploration does not happen in the back seat of a car with two teens touching and feeling and fumbling around in the dark. Neither does it happen with the two of you sneaking around looking for a place where you can "do it." It might work for one (or even both) of you physically, but it is not going to work for you emotionally.

Men and women are made differently—physically, psychologically, and emotionally. Are you listenin', darlin?

Think of sex as a journey that a female might take. Let's say she's traveling the East Coast of the United States. She starts in Maine (her mind) and her journey will end in Florida (intercourse). Foreplay (preparation for intercourse) begins in Maine as she thinks about the male with whom she will have sex. Nine times out of ten she will have

97

thoughts about their relationship: How is it progressing? Is it progressing? Is there a relationship to progress? She'll think about their level of communication, etc.

By the time she gets to Rhode Island, she is thinking about her feelings about him: How does she feel when they are together? What does he do that makes her feel special and loved? Are there any disagreements? What are they about? Does she feel happy? Does she like him? Does he like her? How does he act toward her? etc.

By the time she gets to New Jersey, she's thinking about the kinds of questions she wants to ask (it's the alarm system!) but is afraid to ask...things such as: Why should I have sex with this guy? Does he respect me? How much do I know about him? Will he call tomorrow? What will he think of me? What will *I* think of me? This is a pretty stressful situation for the female. There isn't too much pleasure going on, is there?

By the time she reaches Virginia, if the answers to these questions are coming back negative, the trip to Florida is canceled! In other words, a female's thoughts and feelings are so much a part of her sexual experience that if the vast majority of those components are not positive (mind and emotions), she will not be sexually stimulated, aroused, or even interested in having sex.

Conversely, males in our culture have been bombarded with images of females as sexual objects. Many have been convinced that the sexual journey is not a journey at all but a trip that begins and ends in Florida ("intercourse"), a trip to be made as often as possible with as many different partners as possible. What's more, such behavior is touted as proving manhood. Too many young black males have not seen responsible behavior toward females modeled by others in their lives; they tend to grow up surrounded by this "player" sexual mindset. Seeing little to contradict this model, they accept it as correct—that casual sex does not damage them but enhances them as men. Darlin', is Satan selling tickets on this one or what?

The real deal, darlin', is that *both* males and females are missing the boat on this one. When young women *and men* lose their virginity as a result of engaging in casual sex, both suffer a kind of disconnect from themselves. We experience feelings of guilt, shame, anger, vulnerability, loneliness, and fear (contrast 1 John 4:18). They feel as if a part of them has been drained away or removed, and instinctively they know that they can never get it back. Yes, God has the power to forgive our mistakes and bad judgment calls. Still, we know our sense of wholeness is gone. (My darlin', do you really want your whole sense of self riding on a phone call that may or may not come the day after?) Think about some of the young women you have seen on television talk shows discussing their feelings of shame and guilt after casual sex. Do they look happy and fulfilled to you?

Again, it is within marriage that God wants couples to begin their journeys of sexual discovery together. It is within marriage that both partners grow to learn, to give, to share, to anticipate, and to be sensitive to each other's needs. It is within marriage that the questions should not arise.

God does not want this act of sexual giving to be cheapened, taken for granted, or entered into casually. The sexual act brings two people together as one (1 Corinthians 6:17). Remember that God already has the one picked out for you.

The story of Jacob and Esau is told in Genesis 27. Esau was to be given the birthright, the ultimate gift from a father to an elder son. There was only one gift and he was to have it, but he failed to appreciate its value. In a moment of weakness, he simply gave it away in exchange for dinner. When he fully realized what he had done, he was devastated, but it was too late.

My darlin', your virginity, your sexuality is as precious to God as the birthright was to Esau. It is God's gift to you. Don't ignore or underestimate its value, for it is priceless. It is not a prize to be given to the "lucky guy" who whispers the right sweet nothings in your ear. It is not a reward for the guy who demonstrates the most persistence in whining, begging, and wearing you down. Neither is it a litmus test of how far you are willing to go to prove loyalty, womanhood, strength, or love. (Reread Chapter 6, girl! Your love security system needs a tune-up!)

No, my darlin', your sexuality is the ultimate part of you that is to be given in love and cherished till death. Don't surrender it in exchange for a date—whether it comes with dinner or not!

A Prayer for You

Dear God,

There is a tidal wave of lies, deceit, and misinformation about sex and sexuality aimed directly at this child and her peers. So much of this world does not speak peace to her at all, but pulls and tugs at her spirit to go in every direction except for the direction that leads to you. It's a wide road, God, and so often it is easy to get overwhelmed by the crowd on the road or to get washed away by the tidal wave.

Teach her, Lord, that you are her anchor in the time of storm, her roadmap on the journey of life. Breathe on her and snatch her back from the grip of those who would mislead her into thinking that the giving of her body is "no big thing" or that it leads to "building a relationship." Open her ears and her eyes so that she will recognize this lie whenever she hears it, from whoever says it! Keep her alarm system on, ready and in working order to shield and protect her. Help her, Father, to be strong so that she will choose to listen and respond obediently to her alarm system. Teach her to respect it, to have gratitude for it, and to never turn it off.

Raise up in her Spirit the truth—that you have made her too smart, too special, and too loved to settle for less than the best...that which you have created and set aside especially for her.

Speak truth and peace to her. Constantly remind her that she is not crazy, stupid, uptight, frigid, cold, weird, or less than a woman when she chooses to live in obedience to your Word. Bless her, Lord, and all of her days. In Jesus' name, I pray. Amen.

For Your Consideration

1. Read Genesis 27. How does this story about Jacob and Esau relate to young people today?
2. Locate and read a copy of the traditional marriage vows. How important do you think they are?

A Prayer from You

. . .

18

FEAR

WHOM ARE YOU WORSHIPING?

Thou shalt have no other gods before me. Thou shalt not bow down thyself to them, nor serve them: for I the LORD *thy God am a jealous god visiting the iniquity [sin] of the fathers upon the children unto the third and fourth generation of them that have me. (Exodus 20:3-5, KJV)*

My Dear One,

If you read a newspaper on any given day, you probably won't be able to go far before you see an article about domestic violence. Until recently, most people have thought of it as being a problem that involved only adults—married couples or at least folks in some kind of live-in arrangement. However, recent law enforcement statistics (and TV talk shows) now indicate that this violence is being experienced by teenage girls. We hear and see horror stories of teen girls who are being stalked, kidnapped, slapped, beaten, isolated from family and friends, and in the worst cases, killed—by boyfriends.

Quite often, these female victims say many similar things: that she loves the guy; she has tried to please him and not anger him; she is afraid of what he can do and will do; that the guy is controlling and manipulative. These victims have invariably tried to become the person the male wanted them to be and have said that the male is their whole world. This, my darlin', is very dangerous ground because it is territory where Satan thrives.

The real deal is this: To make a human (or anything else) the center of your universe and source of everything is to make an idol of that person or thing. He gets all of your attention, time, and focus. You may not see it this way, but you do make sacrifices to him, not only of your body, but of your sense of self-esteem, your capacity to love and be loved by him. You make yourself a servant, slave, "punching bag," and idol worshiper. Your temple becomes polluted when you bring in something, someone that should not be there. No wonder these relationships are so destructive!

The Ten Commandments make perfectly clear what God thinks about those who would have such a dominant place in our lives...in the places that only God should dwell (our temples). "Thou shalt have no other gods before me" (Exodus 20:3, KJV), and God is not playing! God plays second to *no one!* Further, the Lord says, "you shall not bow down to them or worship them; for I, the LORD your God, am a jealous God" (Exodus 20:5, NIV).

God begs you to remember a few things if you ever find yourself being lured into this kind of destructive relationship.

First, don't allow Satan to play you like that! He plays on your ignorance of God's Word. Proverbs 29:11 says, "A fool gives full vent to his anger, but a wise man keeps himself under control." God does not want his daughters paired up with fools who take out their anger on you. (Turn your alarm system on full blast, girl!)

Second, learn God's definition of love for yourself. Satan takes advantage of the fact that since you don't know God's definition, he can present anything to you, call it love, and you will accept it. Think about what many popular songs and movies are saying about it. Is that really love?

Third, understand that abusive relationships are toxic. They destroy everything and everyone involved. Satan wouldn't have it any other way. He wants you to believe that you are smart enough, sexy enough, and loving enough to change this guy and his behavior. My darlin', God is the only one who can change a demon into one of his children. Don't fool yourself, waste your time, or get your feelings hurt. The only thing that you can do is pray for this brother, leave him in the hands of the Lord, and get on with the things that God wants you to do.

My darlin', choose to believe what God says is true. Don't start one, won't be one! If you don't attempt to start a relationship with these guys, there won't be a relationship. And, you won't become a statistic. Be cautious of those who are quick-tempered (both males and females) and prone to aggressive, unnecessarily forceful, and violent behavior, yet speak words of care, concern, and love (James 3:10-11). Be alert and keep your eyes wide open. Obey the Spirit's warnings when that voice inside you says to stay away. (That alarm system is going crazy, girl!) These kinds of behaviors destroy all concerned and become barriers to you and your relationship to God. They please only Satan, for he would have you believe that you don't need the love and protection of God. Spit in his eye and call on God—always.

A Prayer for You

Father God,

Your Word tells us that Satan is a liar and a deceiver. He would have us think that love comes in the form of physical and emotional pain from anger and fear by the hands of another. Lead your daughter to your Word where she can stay rooted and grounded, so that she can recognize the lies and deceit from Satan when she sees and hears them—especially in matters of the heart.

I pray for her as she ventures out into the world that you have made but that Satan has so carefully twisted. Help her to see clearly the wrong that he calls right and the right that he calls wrong. Open her mouth that she would cry out to you for wisdom, courage, and strength. If she would be tempted to stray into "wolf" territory, because you are her Shepherd, take the crook of your staff and lead her back to your fold and your protection.

Give her wisdom and a discerning spirit as she chooses her friends and associates. I know you will be there to guide and direct her, but give her the assurance of your presence.

I also pray now, Lord, for those who would become her friends and special interests. I ask your presence in their lives as well. May you be the source of their worship, honor, and reverence. In Jesus' name, we pray. Amen.

For Your Consideration

1. Read James 1:19-20. How does this apply to people you know? How does this apply to you?
2. Read Ephesians 4:26. How does this apply to you?
3. Read 2 Timothy 1:7. What does this passage have to do with relationships?

A Prayer from You

. . .

19

DON'T BELIEVE THE HYPE!

*Can anything separate us from the love of Christ?
Can trouble, suffering, and hard times, or hunger
and nakedness, or danger and death? In everything
we have won more than a victory because of Christ
who loves us. I am sure that nothing can separate us
from God's love—not life or death, not angels or
spirits, not the present or the future, and not powers
above or powers below. Nothing in all creation can
separate us from God's love for us in Christ Jesus our
Lord! (Romans 8:35-39, CEV)*

My Dear One,

Quite a few years ago, a small, suburban town in New Jersey
experienced a terrible series of deaths. An investigation
revealed that teenagers were making suicide pacts and then
carrying them out. Parents and school administrators were
shocked to learn that teens were choosing death over life for
all kinds of reasons: boyfriend/girlfriend problems, lack of
self-esteem, family troubles, problems with parents, academic

and school problems, etc. The whole town, as well as the nation, was in shock; families were totally devastated. For months following the deaths, authorities remained cautious and questioned the possibility of "copycat" deaths by teens in other parts of the country.

It is amazing the way Satan creates pictures in our minds of how horrible our lives, our problems are. The ways he can twist and wrap us up in fear, self-pity, and hopelessness! The ways he works to convince folks that suicide is an easy way out and the answer to their problems.

Remember the Walt Disney movie *Snow White and the Seven Dwarfs*? Remember the scene where Snow White eats the poisoned apple and dies and the dwarfs take her body and encase it in glass? The dwarfs and all of the forest animals stand around and mourn her. Some people (of all ages) think that suicide is very much like the scene from that movie: that their self-inflicted death will cause all life to stand still and be sorrowful; that friends and family will mourn forever. Suicide has been romanticized and fantasized.

My darlin', Satan would have you think that way, and you would think wrong.

The real deal is that suicide is a way of telling God that he is a liar and a cheat. It tells God that he is not who the Word says he is; that God is not all-knowing or all-powerful. In fact, it is a way of saying that God is powerless to act on our behalf, that God is ineffective against those who would wrong us, and that God cannot protect us from evil. And worst of all, it tells God that he cannot be trusted. It is an assault on God's reputation.

Oh, my darlin', when a person chooses (and it is a choice) to believe those kinds of things about our Creator, our Heavenly Father, the one who loves us so dearly, it breaks God's heart and makes Satan very happy. Satan rejoices in our confusion, anger, and bitterness. The enemy wants us to act on those feelings. Satan wants us to think that death by suicide is our only way out of pain, fear, and suffering.

It has been said that it is Satan's job "to make God regret that he ever made us." God's Word warns us to "be on your guard and stay awake. Your enemy, the devil, is like a roaring lion, sneaking around to find someone to attack. But you must resist the devil and stay strong in your faith" (1 Peter 5:8-9, CEV). But Scripture then gives assurance by promising that "you will suffer for awhile, but God will make you complete, steady, strong, and firm. God will be in control forever" (1 Peter 5:10-11, CEV).

That promise also applies to the family members who are left to deal with the hurt and pain of those who have chosen suicide. True, parents and family members will be hurt and mourn the loss; some will never get over it. But, slowly and in time, they will get up in the morning and learn how to continue to live their lives—without that person. They will learn to ask God for the strength to endure, and the Lord will give them all that they will need—the same way God will give you strength if and when you ask him.

God removes all hurt and pain, no matter what has caused it. But, you must ask him and you must believe that he can do it. You must also realize that God allows pain and suffering in order to teach you about endurance, strength, and courage—many of the things your temple needs in order to stand. Give God time to work his miracle of strength in you. Choose to believe that God is all that God says he is!

When things begin to pile up and you feel overwhelmed, frustrated, and lost, take a breath. Go to your own personal, private space and have yourself a good cry—a real good cry. It is important that you feel the pain and acknowledge it, so that you can throw it right back in Satan's face!

Take a nice long bath or shower and then get on your knees (or your bed or a chair) and have a real long heart-to-heart with God. (He's your friend, remember?) Be honest with God and lay it on the line. He's a big God and can take it. Tell the Lord that you are hurt and disappointed. Tell God that you are leaving your problems in his care and that you are expecting him to take them on. Get that neck action going (like when you get that attitude, girl!), and get up in God's face—just like the rappers are up in the cameras in the videos! Remind God of all his promises to you: that he loves you, cares for you, will neither leave you nor forsake you. And tell God you are holding him to those promises. Remind God of his reputation. Get God told real good. Then after you finish talking, don't get up and leave, because the conversation is only halfway completed. Continue to sit, be quiet, and let God talk to *you*. Listen for his views on your situation.

Second Corinthians 4:7-9 tells us, "The real power comes from God and not from us. We often suffer, but we are never crushed. Even when we don't know what to do, we never give up. In times of trouble, God is with us, and when we are knocked down, we get up again" (CEV). God tells us to test him, to try him out. In times of despair, my darlin', do just that!

And, let Satan know that you saw the end of the movie. Snow White, with the aid of the prince, wakes up from her *sleep* (not her death!) and goes on to live a happy life.

A Prayer for You

Our Father in Heaven,

Teach your daughter to look to you for courage and strength when she is hurting and in pain...confused and angry, frustrated and bitter, hopeless and in despair. Help her to seek you first. Breathe on her and let her feel your presence. Relax and calm her down. Forgive her doubts and fears about you.

Teach her to thank you for giving her tears that can be shed during trying times. Thank you for allowing her to feel pain, so that she may be more considerate and caring of others who are hurting. Lead and guide her to share with others all the ways you have comforted, restored, and loved her.

Father, teach her how to pray for herself as well as those who do not know you—for those who allow Satan free rein in their lives. I know that you will listen to her prayers as she comes to you for others as well as herself.

Help her to stay mindful of her times of doubt and weakness *and* of the times when she has felt your presence in her life, guiding her, changing her, making her better. Keep her mind clear and alert, her heart entrusted to you, and her spirit clean and focused.

I pray that she will seek you in all things. I know you will hear her as she cries out to you, and when she is quiet and listening you will speak truth and peace to her spirit. In Jesus' name, I pray. Amen.

For Your Consideration

1. Read Ecclesiastes 3:1-12. What does this passage teach you about change?

2. Read 2 Corinthians 12:7-10. Make a list of the "thorns" in your flesh. What is your plan for dealing with them?

A Prayer from You

■ ■ ■

20

LACK OF CONFIDENCE IN GOD

LET DAD MAKE IT BETTER

Is he not your Father, your Creator, who made you and formed you? (Deuteronomy 32:6b, NIV)

Cast all your anxiety on him because he cares for you. (1 Peter 5:7, NRSV)

My Dear One,
Rev. Keith Cook, my husband, once preached a sermon called "The Beginning of Manhood." He listed the difficulties in trying to teach young men what it meant to be real men, men of God. He talked about all of the physical and cultural signs of African American boys becoming men: growing a beard and chest hair, voice changing, growth spurts, recognizing one's sexuality, having sex while still teens, fathering children but not becoming fathers, going to jail or prison, etc.

Our society has not been a friend to African American males, our marriages, or our families. In fact, marriage suffers greatly in our culture for everybody! The divorce rate soars (currently, one out of two marriages end in divorce), and alarming numbers of children are growing up without the benefit of having two committed parents in the marriage or in the home.

Situations like these can be extremely damaging to children. Many grow up without a sense of the marriage design that God intended. They don't see their fathers being the provider, protector, and spiritual leader of their families. Neither do they see their mothers being provided for, protected, or serving as spiritual support. Mothers are called on to play both roles, and fathers are too often simply not a presence in their children's lives. Many children grow up thinking of fathers as uncaring, unreliable, insensitive, and absent. They grow up feeling unworthy of their father's time, attention, concern, and love. Some grow up angry, bitter, and frustrated.

This is dangerous ground, for Satan thrives here.

My darlin', the real deal is that Satan plays on these feelings of pain and abandonment by convincing children that they are flawed to the point of being unlovable. He tells them that males in general (and fathers specifically) cannot be trusted, and therefore comfort and support must be found in other places (e.g., drugs, alcohol, crime, same-sex relationships, promiscuity, relationships with older men, gangs, etc.). He pushes them into feeling that love is expressed only through material gifts or by physical touch.

The story is told of a young woman who had suffered greatly at the hands of males in her life—an abusive stepfather, a troubled first marriage, and a difficult second marriage. She found it difficult to pray to God, whom Scripture and church tradition most often describe in masculine language or images (e.g., king, father, husband). She is not unique in her feelings.

There are many young people who find it hard to relate to God as their Father because of the damaged relationships with their earthly fathers. Too often, they agree with Satan's distorted version of fatherhood.

Oh, my darlin', how this breaks God's heart!

As humans, we receive our first sense of what it means to be totally dependent on someone for love, care, and protection from our parents...particularly from our fathers. When he (or a significant male role model) is missing, we can become confused and begin to accept what Satan says. We begin to think that if our earthly fathers are not here for us (and we can see them), how then can we rely on a heavenly Father whom we can't see? (Satan stays busy, doesn't he?)

Well, darlin', that's a mistake a lot of folks make.

God's Word (and you must choose to believe it) tells us that before there was anything, there was God. He created this world, everything in it—especially you—and called it good. You, like the rest of us, were made in God's image with all of his characteristics—laughter, tears, the ability to love and be loved, etc. But, unlike human beings, God is perfect and cannot make mistakes. Therefore, we cannot afford to think of God or treat him as if he were just another human being. God describes himself in Isaiah 55:8-9 like this: "'For my thoughts are not your thoughts, neither are your ways my ways,' declares the LORD. 'As the heavens are higher than the earth so are my ways higher than your ways and my thoughts than your thoughts'" (NIV).

My darlin', there is something so wonderful and awesome to know that God is not like us…that God is so much more than humans could ever be. That is why it is so important that you learn to grow out of dependence on earthly parents, because we are limited in the things that we can do for you—and at times, we fall short…really short! We hurt and disappoint you. We sometimes fail to provide for your needs. Darlin', you are to mature from looking to us for most things to looking to God for all things. It is called growing into dependence—total dependence and reliance—on God, who is unlimited and will never disappoint you. Psalm 27:10 says, "Though my father and mother forsake me, the LORD will receive me" (NIV). Think about it. God says, "When your parents mess up their lives or don't do the job that I have told them to do with you, don't worry. I'm here and I've always got your back!"

In other words, God is not just the keeper of your temple; God is also your Father, your Dad, your Source. He's the father that provides, protects, leads, and guides you. God is the dad whom you confide in, cry to, and trust with everything in your life. God is the source who owns everything and, therefore, can supply your every need. God's the dad who brings you laughter and the father who is quick to forgive when you really mess up. He's the dad who loves you, even when you find it hard to love yourself, and the father who will stand right by your side as you learn life's lessons—sometimes the hard way.

And, God's the dad who drives folks nuts bragging about you, his beautiful, talented, wonderful, fantastic child! You are God's daughter, a chip off of his block, the one with the incredibly bright future ahead of her. (Remember, God has plans for you!)

What a great guardian of your temple! What a great father...what a dad, and what a blessed daughter!

A Prayer for You

Our Father, who lives in heaven and with us here on earth,

The world has gone crazy in its definitions of what it means to be a man, a father. You have told us to call *you* Father because, among so many other things (creator, provider, friend, healer, and confidante) you are our dad. As your children, we are so grateful that you are not limited to what we can see, hear, taste, and touch, like earthly fathers. You are so far above and beyond that. You are real power, healing power, the power of love.

Father, as your daughter ventures out into the world that you have made but we have messed up, guide her footsteps. Remind her that you are the father in the story of the prodigal son (Luke 15) and that you will never tire of running out to meet her when she comes running to you for forgiveness, guidance, direction, and a renewed spirit of obedience to you. Always remind her that nothing she could ever do—nothing—separates her from your love, your forgiveness. If she will but ask, believing, it will be done. Satan can make her *think* that a separation from your love is possible, but that is all that he can do. He is a liar, and he is wrong.

Give her wisdom and understanding to know that she cannot take on the problems of those around her, for she cannot save anyone—not even herself. But teach her to call on you for mercy, grace, and your saving power for herself, her family, her friends, and associates.

And when the time comes that you have selected and set aside for her to have boyfriends, relationships, love, and marriage, breathe on her so that she will be guided to those who have been set aside for her. Give her patience and calm and the assurance that since you are her father, her dad, she can trust your decisions completely, because she knows you want only the best for her life. She is yours and you are hers, and nothing can change that. I pray this prayer for your daughter, your child, your dear and precious one. In Jesus' name. Amen.

For Your Consideration

1. Read Luke 15. What does this passage teach you about youth? About wisdom? About repentance? About God's grace?
2. If you were asked to role-play the part of the father in this parable, could you? Why or why not?

A Prayer from You

. . .

LAST PART

THE
REAL
DEAL

ON FINISHING TOUCHES
FOR YOUR TEMPLE

CONCLUSION

Now to him who is able to keep you from falling, and to make you stand without blemish in the presence of his glory with rejoicing, to the only God our Savior, through Jesus Christ our Lord, be glory, majesty, power and authority, before all time and now and forever. Amen. (Jude vv. 24-25, NRSV)

Rolling Out the Welcome Mat!

Well, my darlin', is this it? Everything you need to assist you on your way to womanhood? All the tools needed to build your temple of the spirit? Hardly. I've barely scratched the surface. Let's just say I've tried to make a major impression as you begin to dig the ground for the foundation of your temple.

There are some things that I've said over and over to the point of redundancy. I don't apologize for it; I'm just desperately trying to emphasize certain points. So, one more time, here's the real deal about God—and you.

■ God does love you and has so many wonderful things in store for you and you alone. No one, *no one* can take from you what God has set aside just for you. Make the choice to believe that.

- The Book of Ecclesiastes is right: It is imperative that you remember your Creator while you are young.

- You must build a relationship—friend, confidante, provider, healer, child—with God the Father and his Son, Jesus Christ, so you might grow daily in the knowledge of God.

- God does not demand that you live a life of perfection but one of holiness—reading, following, and living in obedience to his Word.

- In spite of what the world says, becoming a woman is a *process* of physical, psychological, emotional, and spiritual growth and development.

- You have only one temple of the mind, body, and spirit. Build it carefully, filling it with the richness of God's grace, the fullness of his love, and gratitude to his Son for doing for you that which you can never do for yourself—save you from sin.

- Finally, the Old Testament Book of Micah holds words that should be placed over the entrance to your temple: "The LORD has told us what is right and he demands: 'See that justice is done, let mercy be your first concern, and humbly obey your God'" (6:8, CEV).

The final act of a contractor completing a building project is to present the new owner with the keys to the property. It is then and only then that the owner is assured of the freedom to occupy the building.

So it is with God, who waits for you to turn over the keys to your temple so that the Holy Spirit can claim ownership. God can do that only when you declare Jesus Lord of your life.

My dear one, an old Negro spiritual says,
I'm workin' on a building,
It's a sure foundation.
I'm holdin' up the blood-stained banner for my Lord.
As soon as I get through
Workin' on the building,
I'm going up to heaven to get my reward.
Build sure. Build solid. Build joyfully. The Holy Family awaits occupancy.

A Prayer for You

Father God,

There are no words for the joy and peace that you give us when we know who and what you are in our lives. I ask that this child, your daughter, learn that same joy, peace, confidence, and assurance as she grows into womanhood. I know that you love her and pray that she comes to know and love you.

You have told us to pray without ceasing. Give us all strength that we may live in obedience to you and to do just that. It is in the blessed name of Jesus I ask all things. Amen.

And that, my darlin', is THE REAL DEAL!